The Country Life Book for
The Young Rider

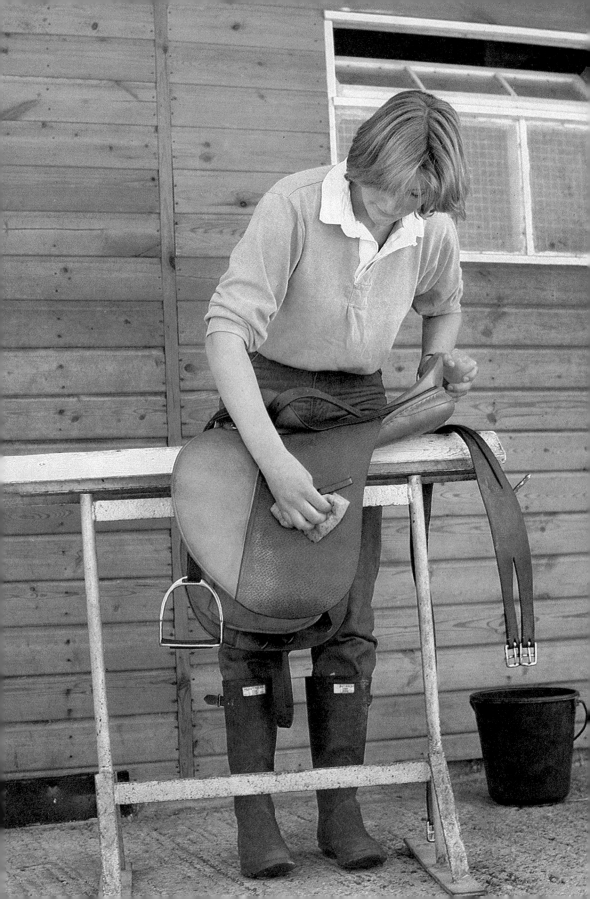

The Country Life Book for
The Young Rider

Robert Owen
John Bullock

COUNTRY LIFE
BOOKS

Acknowledgements

The authors are grateful to Bob Langrish who has provided many of the illustrations used in this book. Those used on pages 94–99 are from Jon Whitbourne.

by the same authors

Robert Owen
My Learn to Ride Book
Successful Riding and Jumping
Learning to Ride
The Country Life Book of the Horse (editor)
Riding and Jumping
Horse and Pony Dictionary

John Bullock
The Horse and Pony Quiz Book
Care of the Horse

Robert Owen and John Bullock
Buying and Keeping a Horse or Pony
Caring for a Horse or Pony
Riding and Schooling
About Jumping
The Country Life Book of Horse and Rider
Newnes All Colour Guide: Riding

Published by Country Life Books
an imprint of the Hamlyn Publishing Group Limited,
Bridge House, 69 London Road, Twickenham,
Middlesex, England, and distributed for them by
The Hamlyn Publishing Group Limited,
Rushden, Northants, England.

ISBN 0 600 33393 0

Printed in Spain

Contents

Preface

Before 1930 very few books of instruction had been written specifically for the young rider. One of the earliest and most successful, The Young Rider, *was published by Country Life in 1928.*

After having been reprinted twice a revised edition was produced in 1931, and a third edition, this time extensively revised and enlarged, followed in 1935.

The third edition remained in print throughout the years of the second world war, but such were the changes and developments in post-war years that yet another edition was published in 1952.

During 1974, with the fourth edition long out of print, Country Life decided that a completely new book of instruction, using the title The Young Rider, *should be commissioned. Ideally, this was to follow the pattern of the earlier editions, though with so many new approaches to teaching and horsemanship it was recognised that a completely new book would emerge.*

Robert Owen and John Bullock, both of whom have written many books on equestrian subjects, were invited to prepare the new volume. The completely new book was published under the original title in the Spring of 1976. The impact was immediate and the book was well received at home and in many countries throughout the world.

The authors derive particular satisfaction in knowing that they keep alive a well-known and well-loved title. They are also aware that many of today's younger riders have grandparents and parents who were brought up on earlier editions, and earnestly hope all who ride, and those yet to learn to ride, will find much to enjoy in this, the sixth edition of The Young Rider.

R.O.
J.B.

1
About buying

AT SOME STAGE in your riding career you may be in the happy
position of thinking about buying your own horse or pony, and
when this time comes you must make sure you are prepared to
devote the necessary time, energy and money required to look
after it. Owning a horse or pony, with all the attending demands
made on you, will be one of the most rewarding of occupations -
but only if you are fully prepared to put the animal's welfare in
front of your own.

But, finding a suitable horse or pony can prove to be a most
time consuming business and, therefore, it is important first of all
to establish the type you are looking for.

A first horse should be quiet and reliable, whether it is
intended for a child or an adult. Experience and temperament are
more important than looks at this stage, as these attributes will
help instil confidence in a beginner or novice rider and provide a
suitable stepping stone on which to learn.

Another factor to consider is where the animal is to be kept.

A Thoroughbred-type, not necessarily a one hundred percent
Thoroughbred, will be unable to cope with living out all year
round, and will require to spend more time in the stable than at
grass. On the other hand, a native bred pony will be happier
living out in the open throughout the year.

It is also important to find a horse or pony which is the right
size for the rider. Never buy a horse that is too big, thinking that
one might grow into it. A horse that is too large will invariably
prove too strong to be easily managed, and will become difficult
to handle and a nuisance to ride. Yet being under-horsed, having a
horse or pony which is too small, can be as much of a
disadvantage. Try to find an animal that is big enough to carry
you easily without being too large to control.

Buying a young horse for a beginner or inexperienced rider is never a good idea and can lead to all manner of disasters. An older animal, which is reliable and sensible enough to be ridden on its own, or in company with other horses and ponies, will provide far more enjoyment and satisfaction.

When choosing a horse or pony bear in mind the job you will want it to do. A showjumper who has performed well for one rider may not go so well for another – even though their experience may be roughly identical. Look for a horse that has shown proven ability in the activity you intend to pursue, or one that has shown itself to be a good, sound all-rounder.

Having decided on the type, size and age of animal, where do you begin to look?

It is worth making an approach to a local riding school or equestrian establishment for advice. They sometimes have horses and ponies for sale. If they do not, or should you decide not to consider a horse that has been used in a school, ask if they can recommend a reputable dealer. A good dealer of horses and ponies, and there are many, will be careful to safeguard his reputation, and will often exchange an animal should the first choice prove to be unsuitable.

Many horses are sold at auctions and, depending on the nature of any warranty given, these can be returned to the vendor within a stipulated period of time should they be unsound. Buying at horse sales is always something of a gamble, though it is a common practice in many countries throughout the world.

At the end of the day it is usually found that good horses are nearly always sold privately, giving the purchaser an opportunity to see and test the horse on offer, and allowing the vendor to get to know something about the home their horse will be going to.

Many local newspapers, and most of the national equestrian magazines, carry 'horses for sale' columns. But for those buying for the first time it is recommended they place their own worded advertisement in a 'horses wanted' column. In this the buyer should state the exact requirements, requesting replies which should give size, age, type or breed, experience and performance, and a photograph if possible. The prospective buyer will then look through all replies, picking out the most suitable, and begin looking at those which are situated nearest to home.

But, whichever way you plan to buy, especially should this be for the first time, it is wise to seek the advice of a knowledgeable and experienced friend. There are many pitfalls awaiting the prospective buyer, and someone with experience might well be in a position to spot any queries regarding soundness, temperament or suitability.

Left: a group of four riders under instruction. It can be seen how well the horses and riders are turned-out. *Below:* Welsh ponies enjoy a supplementary feed of hay in their snow-covered paddock.

When you look at a horse or pony for the first time, see it first in its stable. Watch how it reacts to people, notice whether it is nervous, bad tempered or disinterested in the proceedings. Look for the horse with a kind eye and alert expression, and one that stands quietly and shows no signs of fear or anxiety. Next, it is important to see him trotted up in hand. Make sure he moves with a straight gait and is sound.

Always ask to see the animal ridden before trying him yourself. When looking at a horse or pony for the purpose of jumping, notice how he goes over a few obstacles before you get mounted. See that he does not 'hot up'. Pay careful attention to his behaviour: whether or not he is relaxed and obedient, or shows signs of having bad manners.

Horses for inexperienced riders should always be good in

Below: a horse and pony standing side-by-side to show the difference in size. Ponies usually stand up to 14.2 hh, though in some showing classes ponies standing up to 15 hh are accepted.

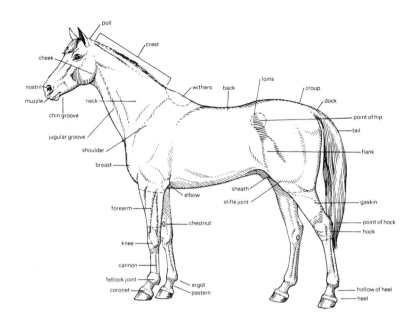

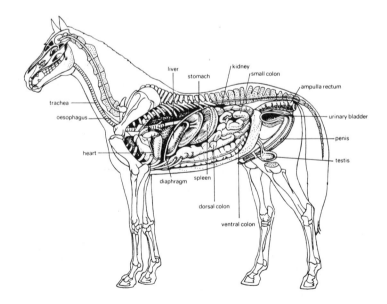

Above: the points of the horse.

Left: the anatomy of the horse.

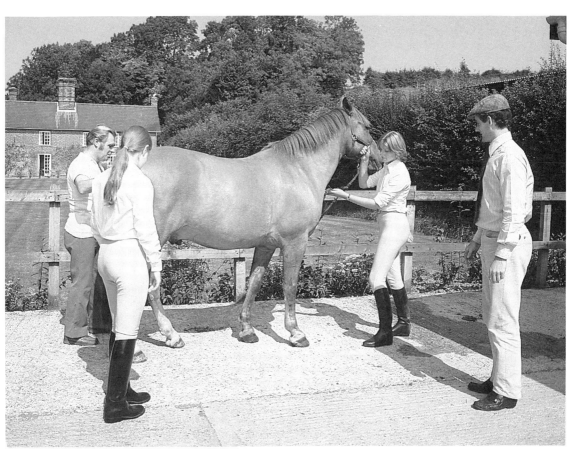

Above: a close examination is essential before considering whether or not to buy. This should be carried out before asking to see the horse or pony being ridden out. The buyer's veterinary surgeon will later be asked to carry out a full inspection and to prepare a report.

traffic, particularly should you have to exercise him on or near roads and highways. Have him ridden out of the yard and taken along any adjacent road. There is nothing more dangerous, or worrying, than a horse or pony which is traffic-shy.

Whatever type of horse or pony you finally decide to buy you *must* ensure it is properly vetted. Your own veterinary surgeon will be able to advise you whether or not the animal is in a suitable condition for your requirements, which of course you will have previously discussed with him. His report will show whether the horse or pony is sound in eyes, heart, wind and limb.

Finding the right horse or pony may take several weeks or months. Do not become disheartened should you fail to find the one you are seeking straight away. Never buy in haste or desperation.

Always be prepared to accept advice. Choose carefully and according to your experience and requirements. Take your time, and listen to all that your veterinary surgeon has to say.

Hopefully, in the end, you will find exactly the horse or pony you have been looking for, and will become the owner of an animal who will give tremendous pleasure and satisfaction and many hours of complete enjoyment.

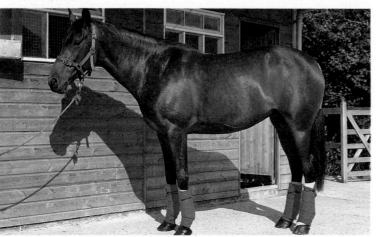

Above: the veterinary surgeon will have a horse or pony trotted up towards him as part of his routine inspection.

Left: good conformation can be spotted by experienced owners and riders. When looking at a horse it is useful to be able to bring to mind the 'points' as illustrated on page 12.

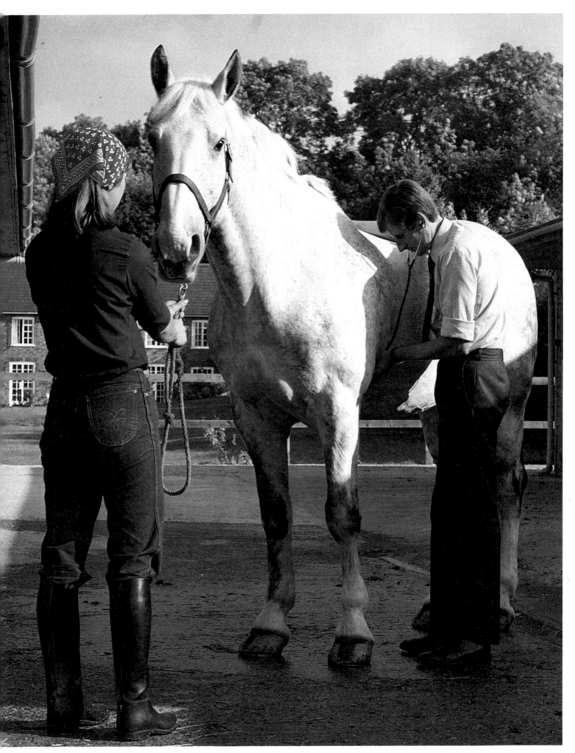

Above: just as a doctor will examine the patient's pulse rate, so the veterinary surgeon always carries out a check of the pulse and respiratory condition of a horse who is either to be purchased or who is known to be sick or lame.

2
The stable-kept horse or pony

THERE ARE TRADITIONALLY four ways of keeping a horse or pony. If you have the necessary facilities at home or near by you can look after him yourself or with the help of the family – or perhaps there may be a groom to look after him for you. If not you will have to keep him at livery at a riding stable, where you will pay a weekly charge for his upkeep. You will, of course, also have to pay the blacksmith and any veterinary bills. He will be exercised for you – and you will be able to ride him when you wish. Some stables can be persuaded to keep ponies at half-livery. This means that the owners of the stables have the use of the pony themselves for riding lessons or hacking during certain times of the week, and the livery charge is reduced accordingly.

Looking after the animal yourself is naturally the most satisfying way of being a horse-owner, but you must be prepared for plenty of hard work over long hours. If you enjoy lying in bed in the morning, then think twice before becoming an owner-rider. You might be better off going to the local stables and riding a horse that somebody else has got ready for you. But if you do you will miss the pleasure and satisfaction of looking after your own horse and developing that bond of friendship and trust which only horse-owners, who have cared for their own animals, can really appreciate.

Keeping and looking after a horse must be a labour of love. He will have to be fed and watered regularly and looked after properly. If he becomes ill you may well have to put his needs before your own.

You may have bought a pony which can be kept out all the year round. Even so there will be times when you will want to bring him into a stable, and need to know how to look after him while he is there.

Unless you are fortunate enough to have a suitable stable yard and loose boxes already available, you will either have to convert an existing building into a stable, build one of your own, or perhaps buy a new one. There are a number of reputable firms who supply prefabricated stables that only need to be assembled. These are made of wood and can be erected in the most suitable

place not only for the comfort and well-being of the horse, but also to provide the easiest method of working from your point of view. Keep in mind the positioning of the muck heap, the distance from the hay and straw barns and the place where you will keep the fodder.

A loose box should be roomy enough for a horse to lie down easily without getting 'cast' – stuck against the wall so that he cannot get up without assistance – and high enough to give plenty of head room. It should measure about 3.5m (12ft) by 3m (10ft) for

Below: sweeping-up and keeping the stable yard clean and tidy is an essential part of the daily routine.

a pony, or 4.25m (14ft) by 3.5m (12ft) for a horse. Larger boxes may look better, but they are more expensive to maintain and horses often seem to get into more trouble in a box that is too large than in one which is just about a comfortable size. The roof should slope away from the stable opening, and the stable doors must be high enough to prevent a horse from throwing his head up and banging his poll (back of his head) on the lintel. It is obviously dangerous for horses to hit their heads, and particular care must be taken to ensure that the roof as well as the door lintel are not too low.

The box should be light, airy and draught-proof because horses are very susceptible to draughts even though they can often withstand extremes of cold. Windows should be high up and preferably not in the side of the box opposite the door where they can create a cross-draught.

The siting of the box is also important. It should be placed on well-drained ground with its back to the prevailing winds, and have a solid floor made either of concrete or bricks. If it is made of concrete, the floor should be ridged slightly to prevent it from

Above: the necessary fittings for a secure stable door.

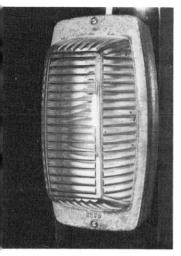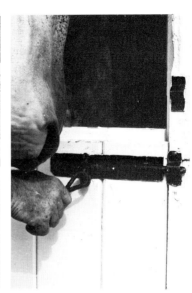

becoming slippery and, because drainage is needed, it should have a gentle slope towards the door with a gully outside.

Doors must be in two parts and open outwards. The top half of the door can be opened to allow the horse to look out and also be fastened with a wall catch to prevent it from banging shut. Good ventilation is important. A grille across the top part of the doorway will allow plenty of fresh air at night without allowing a horse to get out. Ponies in particular can become very clever at getting over the bottom half of a door when no one is about, particularly at night.

The roof must be waterproof. Corrugated iron roofs are noisy in heavy rain and make a stable too warm in hot weather unless properly lined,

There should be as few interior fittings as possible, and there must not be any sharp edges. Mangers with edges are sometimes a problem because horses with a tendency to crib-bite and wind-suck can catch hold of them. For this reason it is wiser to use a strong round feed bowl which the horse cannot knock over and which can be removed for cleaning. There should also be on one of the walls a container to hold a lump of rock salt for the horse to lick.

A strong ring is needed in the wall to which the hay net can be tied high enough to prevent the hay seeds from getting into the horse's eyes and, in addition, there should be room for two water buckets to be placed alongside one of the walls where they can be seen but not easily knocked over. Seeing the buckets every time you enter the stable or look over the door will probably remind you to keep them filled. All electric light fittings and switches should be of the safety variety.

Above: hay rations can be measured more accurately by using a hay net.

A tack room for saddles and bridles, and a fodder store for feeding stuff, should be near by, but hay and straw barns should be some distance away from the stables in case of fire.

The essential needs of every stabled horse are a warm, dry stable, fresh air, exercise, good food of the right type, and plenty of clean water. The best bedding is wheat straw – which should be shaken out and spread knee deep to avoid the risk of capped elbows and hocks. This should be built up a little higher round the sides. It should be kept clean and dry and droppings removed regularly with a skip – hence then term 'skipping out'.

Unless you are using a deep litter the box should be cleaned out thoroughly *every* morning and, providing your horse is not due for early morning exercise, this can be done while he is tied up enjoying his early morning hay net. You will find that he will then stand quietly while you get on with the job.

With a light fork, divide the clean straw from the soiled and pile it in a heap in the corner. The dirty straw and manure can then be taken away to the muck heap. In racing stables the lads

20

Above: the tack room should always be both clean and tidy. Preferably the tack room should be sited adjacent to the stables.

Above: making sure the stable floor is swept clean.

Above: the clean straw is being forked into a corner.

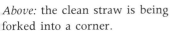

Left: the manure is taken away in a barrow.

often use sacks which have been cut along two sides and opened up to form a square. After the sacks have been filled with the dirty straw the stable lads pick them up with both hands by taking up each corner in turn, and swinging the sack over their shoulders. This is certainly a cheap and easy way of moving wet straw, but it can naturally be messy until you get the knack of picking the sacks up cleanly.

The stable floor should then be thoroughly swept with a hard broom, making sure that the drain is clear. If a box is not going to be used during the day, it can be washed down with a solution of water and disinfectant and then allowed to dry. But if it is required during the day, the clean straw should be spread out

Above: once the mucking-out has been completed, and it is seen that the stable floor is dry, the time comes to put down bedding, adding extra straw to replace that taken away.

Above: wood chips or wood shavings are one of the alternative materials which are used for bedding.

over the floor, and used as a base for fresh straw that will be needed when the horse is bedded down in the evening.

Barley straw is used quite frequently nowadays. As combine harvesters now remove most of the husks and soften up the stalks, there is little to choose between wheat and barley straw providing it is not damp or dusty.

Wood shavings and sawdust have also become popular forms of bedding – particularly if a horse is inclined to have respiratory troubles. This form of bedding is also cheap and easy to handle. Droppings must be removed quickly however, before they can become trodden in, and the wet and dirty patches of bedding must be taken out every morning. A good covering of fresh sawdust or shavings needs to be put down every evening and spread evenly across the centre of the box with a wire rake. It is as well to bank some of the old bedding up round the sides of the walls, about 45cm (18ins) high, to give protection when the horse lies down.

Peat and bracken – and even shredded paper – are other forms of bedding which have been used successfully. Deep litter bedding is a labour-saving method whereby fresh straw is daily laid down over the old straw once the droppings have been picked up and the really wet or dirty straw has been removed. Sawdust is also sometimes used for deep litter.

For deep litter, however, the box must be large and airy. The accumulated litter needs to be cleared out at least every six to eight weeks – and the process started again. As the bed gets deeper the headroom will become less and so you must check that the height from top of the litter to the roof is sufficient. Some owners are keen on the fact that the fermentation which sets up in the deeper layers of the straw generates heat and keeps the whole bed warm. However, there are mixed views on the benefits of deep litter.

The stable timetable must depend on the time you have available *each* day, and can be adapted to suit your individual needs as far as grooming and exercise are concerned. There must, however, be a regular routine. Horses are to a great extent creatures of habit, and they need feeding regularly and at the proper times. If you do not do this you will have neither a happy nor a healthy horse.

The correct way to exercise is dealt with in another chapter, but it is important to stress again that a healthy, active horse needs a steady two hours of exercise a day – mainly walking and trotting, with short periods of cantering on suitable ground once he is really fit.

Regular grooming is, as already said, essential to the health and well-being of every stabled horse or pony because the skin is as vital to an animal's health as are his lungs and heart.

Grooming, known as 'quartering', should be done first thing in the morning. The feet are picked out, the eyes, nostrils and dock are sponged, and the rugs are unbuckled and turned back to allow a quick brush down so that the horse looks tidy before morning exercise.

After a horse has been exercised he will require a thorough grooming or 'strapping'. Because exercise warms up the skin, loosening and raising the scurf to the surface and opening up the pores, it is best to groom after a horse returns from work and is still warm. Grooming is dealt with in more detail in Chapter 6.

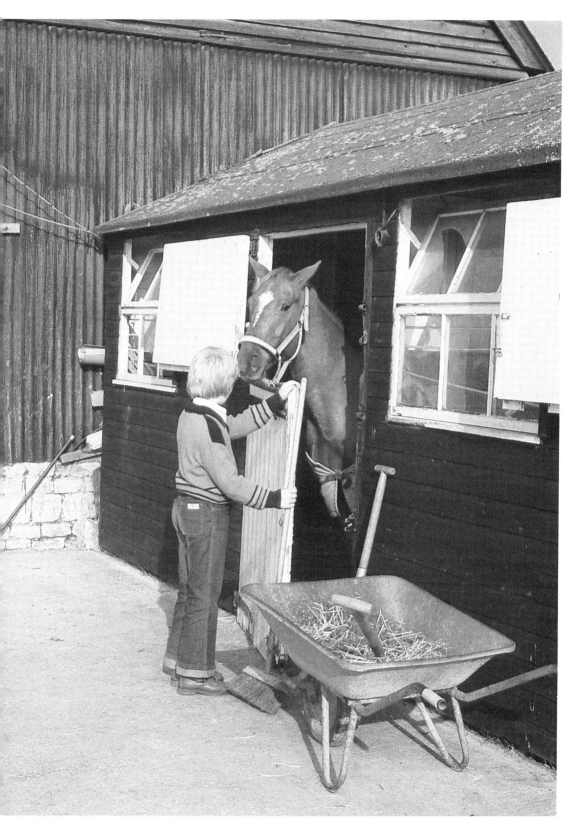

3

Keeping a horse or pony at grass

WHETHER YOU ARE KEEPING a pony out at grass or a Thoroughbred in a stable, there are basic rules to be observed to make sure he remains fit and happy, and that veterinary bills are kept to a minimum. Keeping a horse or pony is never cheap. The larger the animal the more he will cost to feed and stable. Add to that the cost of grazing, fencing, fodder, stable maintenance, tack and travelling, and the inevitable blacksmith's bills, and you will appreciate why it is important to keep other costs – such as visits from your local veterinary surgeon – to within reasonable limits. Many mishaps and illnesses can be prevented by using a little commonsense and forethought.

Every horse or pony kept at grass all the year round should have at least 0.8 hectares of well-fenced and well-drained pasture land. The grass should be neither too lush nor almost bare. Apart from an adequate supply of water, a pony will need a shed to protect him from the elements in winter and the flies in summer, and preferably some sort of stable where he can be taken if he becomes ill or suffers an injury.

Horses and ponies enjoy company and if you are planning to keep only one pony it is a good idea to find out whether anyone else in the area would be prepared to share the grazing, so your pony will have some company. Make sure that the other person's pony is fit and friendly before putting forward the suggestion – if all is well the idea can work quite successfully. If you find the right type of owner they will probably be willing to keep an eye on your pony for you if you have to be away, while you can do the same for them.

If you cannot do this – and you only have one large field for grazing – divide it in two so that one half can be rested while the other half is in use.

Never put a horse or pony into a field unless it is adequately fenced – either by stone walls, thick hedges, or with safe posts and rails about 1.2m (4ft) high. It is also important to ensure that a horse cannot get out on to a road where he can be involved in an accident, or perhaps get on to other land containing trees and plants which may be poisonous.

Ragwort is a common plant in meadows and hedgerows which can prove to be particularly poisonous even after it has been pulled from the ground. For this reason always make sure that you pull out cleanly any ragwort or other poisonous plants you may find in fields. Either burn them or throw the plants away somewhere where they cannot be eaten. Other dangerous plants, trees and shrubs include meadow saffron, horsetails, green bracken, St. John's wort, ground ivy, hemlock, water dropwort, foxgloves, yew, laburnum, rhododendrons, laurel, privet and acacia.

Although part of a large garden can sometimes be fenced-off to make a small paddock for use as an exercising area, ponies will need adequate space in which to graze. Never forget that when a field gets bare the pony will become bored and probably get into trouble.

Ponies never graze close to any of their own dung. You will discover that even though rich-looking clumps of grass grow up round the droppings, ponies will still not graze near them. If the field is small it is wise to pick up the droppings before they can get spread about and ruin a wider area for grazing. Sometimes spreading a layer of cow manure on to a field will counteract the effect of the horse droppings, and encourage the areas to be grazed.

The field will in any case need to be 'topped' frequently with a mowing machine to prevent coarse grass from forming, and to

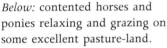

Below: contented horses and ponies relaxing and grazing on some excellent pasture-land.

help promote a sweet, even growth of the shorter grass more attractive to a horse or pony. A few heifers or bullocks will eat the coarser grass and also help to get rid of any red worm left by the horses, but if you do graze cattle always make sure you have really strong fencing because when one bullock or heifer manages to force a gap in a hedge and go through the others will follow.

Sometimes wire fences are inevitable, particularly if cattle are going to graze the fields when horses are not there. The wire, however, should be of plain heavy duty gauge and strained taut with the bottom strand at least a foot from the ground. Barbed wire fencing is not advisable because – apart from the problems of horses getting caught in any loose strands – the barbs can also play havoc with manes and tails.

Below: all riders must know how to open and shut gates when mounted. Teaching the horse or pony to stand still, and be quiet and obedient, is essential.

Gates should be large enough to allow tractors to pass through easily or the field will be difficult to service. All gates should have good catches which are easy to open and close. Ditches in a field can be a problem. The shallow ones are safe enough, but the deeper ones, with straight sides, into which a horse can fall or slide, should be fenced off.

A sound shed is necessary because trees which provide shelter in summer are bare of leaves in the winter and give little protection. The shed needs to be in good order, with plenty of headroom, and roomy enough for horses and ponies to move about freely. It should be placed in such a way as to provide protection from the prevailing winds, but make sure that if horses can get behind the shed there is enough room for them to get out without getting trapped and being hurt. If there is only a narrow gap behind the shed it is safest to fence off the potential trouble area with stout posts and rails.

The roof of the shed should preferably not be made of corrugated iron – which is inclined to get too hot in the summer and will discourage ponies from sheltering underneath at a time when they most need protection from flies. Ensure that the entrance into the shed is wide enough for two full-size horses to pass through together without hurting themselves because, if they do get startled by anything while sheltering there, they may make a dash for the entrance and accidents can then occur.

In the spring the field will require a good harrowing – using a chain harrow to tear up the old grass and moss and let the air into the roots. A few days afterwards it should be rolled in order to even it out and get rid of any ridges and holes which may have been formed during the winter months.

A plentiful supply of clean water can best be provided by an automatic horse trough fitted with a ball-cock to regulate the flow, providing, of course, a piped water supply is laid on to the field. Old baths do not make good water containers because they

Right: a shelter will be a protection in times of bad weather and, in hot weather, a place in which a horse or pony can get away from flies.

Below: fresh water must be available at all times, whether in the stable or in the field or paddock. The best method outdoors is to have this piped to a specially-constructed trough.

are difficult to keep clean and horses are inclined to knock themselves on the rims. Whatever type of water container you use, it should not be placed under any trees where leaves can drop into the water which causes it to become sour. In winter you must break any ice which may have formed.

Water will need to be checked every day to see there is a plentiful supply and nothing has happened to make it undrinkable. It is also a sound practice to walk round fields at regular intervals, not only to check the hedges or fencing but also to make sure that dangerous items like bottles, tins and old plastic containers have not been thrown into it.

Unless a pony is one of the hardier mountain and moorland breeds, you will probably need a New Zealand rug if he is to be kept out in the winter in order to give him protection from the

Some of the plants and shrubs which are dangerous to horses and ponies when the leaves or fruits are eaten in excess include: **1** Kidney vetch; **2** Bracken (when growing); **3** Privet; **4** Oak (acorns); **5** Rhododendron; **6** Yew; **7** Ragwort; **8** Hemlock; **9** Horsetail; **10** Ground ivy; **11** Foxglove; **12** Conifer.

wind and rain. This is a weatherproof, canvas rug which has a surcingle and special leg straps to keep it in place when the animal gets down to roll. New Zealand rugs, however, need to be removed and readjusted morning and evening to prevent any discomfort and galling. It is also important that the rug should fit correctly and be of good quality so that it will not tear easily and lose its waterproofing.

In summer months, some ponies – and particularly those of the mountain and moorland breeds – are susceptible to sweet itch – an irritable condition of the skin which occurs in the region of the crest, withers and croup. The pony can rub raw patches on his mane and tail in an effort to stop the irritation which is basically an allergic condition. It is also thought to be caused by insects of the biting variety. Lotions which can be rubbed into the areas likely to become affected can be quite successful in preventing this miserable condition. There are also mixtures which will bring

Above: the New Zealand rug is made of stout, lined waterproof material. This is perhaps the most widely used of all the rugs required by those who own horses and ponies.

relief once a raw patch has been rubbed. If you see a pony rubbing his mane or tail, act quickly.

Warbles are also a nuisance, particularly in the spring when they develop as lumps beneath the skin on the back, usually in the saddle area. When this happens the maggot of the warble fly will bore a small hole in the skin and then pop out. For this reason, warbles are best left alone until the maggot has made its departure, and then the small hole in the skin can be cleaned and healed by using wound powder or gall ointment. Afterwards, the animal can be ridden by using a numnah with a hole cut to prevent the saddle from touching the affected area. If, however, the maggot is killed while still under the skin, a permanent and troublesome thickening can result. Never ride a horse or pony while a warble is developing.

In some areas bots can be another nuisance in the summer. They appear as little yellow specks on a pony's legs, being caused when the gad fly or bot fly lays eggs on the legs when a pony is in the field. The pony then licks the eggs, swallowing them and transferring them to the stomach where they hatch out. They are not really injurious, but if large quantities of eggs are swallowed in this way the pony can lose condition and develop a rather dry coat.

Most ponies will get bot eggs on their legs when they are out at grass during the summer months. If they are brought into the stable and starved for twenty-four hours, then given a drench made up of two tablespoonsfuls of turpentine to a pint of pure linseed oil, the bots will usually be passed out of the body through the pony's droppings.

Whether a horse or pony is kept at grass or stabled, he will still need to be wormed frequently. Unless they are treated regularly, all ponies will suffer from worms. If this happens they will quickly lose condition, and much of the good food fed to them will be wasted on the worms. There are some sound worming products on the market which can either be mixed with the feed or taken through the mouth by way of a syringe. Your veterinary surgeon will be able to advise you if you are not sure of the best method to use.

Apart from regular visits from the blacksmith, horses and ponies also need their teeth examined at least every twelve months in order to make sure that they have not become too sharp, thus preventing the food from being digested properly. If the teeth are sharp they will need rasping – and this is a job for an expert.

To get the best out of a horse or pony study him carefully and gain his confidence and respect. Every animal is an individual – and should be treated as such.

4
Bringing in a horse or pony from grass

HAVING PURCHASED THE HORSE or pony you feel will suit your needs and got him safely home, you may have had to turn him out into a field. When you go to catch him, however, you might then find that he has decided that he prefers the field – with the freedom it offers – and be determined to stay there.

If you are not sure that a pony will be easy to catch, always take a tit-bit with you, and if you think he may prove really difficult take a small bowl of pony nuts or oats.

Ponies which are difficult to catch should be turned out wearing a headcollar, unless they are going to be out at grass for some length of time. Always remember that the easiest time to catch a pony is when you first approach him. Once he has galloped round the field a few times, and made up his mind not to be trapped, he will be much harder to catch.

Approach from the front or slightly to one side where the pony can see you, and walk towards his shoulder. Trying to creep up on him from behind will only startle him, and you will also be more likely to get kicked.

As you walk slowly, but firmly, towards him, do not forget to talk and encourage him. Give him confidence that there is nothing for him to be worried about.

If he is wearing a headcollar do not make a sudden grab for it when you think you are near enough, but stroke his neck until you can put your fingers through the noseband and slip the rope through the 'D' at the back of the headcollar.

Always use a rope to lead a pony. This is particularly important if you are leading him in traffic. If anything upsets or startles him and he twists away from your grasp, you will not have any chance of controlling him without a rope, and he may get loose in traffic with unfortunate consequences.

Hold the end of the rope with one hand, and take a firm hold of the other end – a short distance from the headcollar – with your other hand, palm downwards.

Unless you are walking along the left-hand side of the road lead from the nearside, that is, the left-hand side of the pony. His right-hand side is called the off side.

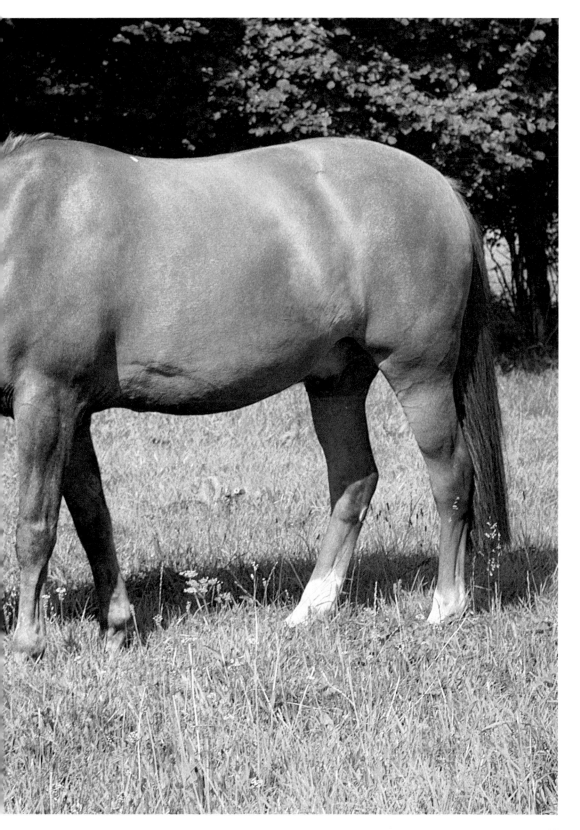

Above: these pictures show a
simple way of tying a quick
release knot which will hold a
pony quite securely.

Above: the string loop will break without damage to the headcollar if the pony pulls sharply away.

To get the pony to move forwards speak to him quietly and walk forward yourself. Always look in the direction in which you want him to go, and not at the pony. Never try to 'pull him along'.

If you want to turn round, make sure that there is nothing coming behind you. Then check his pace, and move him round by pushing his head away from you. In this way the pony will remain balanced, with his head up, and you will be better able to control him.

Left: this clean and well-fitted headcollar is used for both leading and for tying-up.

If the pony does not have a headcollar you will need to use a halter with a rope already attached. After catching your pony, loosen the noseband of the halter and pass the rope gently over his neck, speaking quietly to him as you do so. Then slip the noseband up over his muzzle, and the headpiece over his ears. Tie a knot on the leading side where the rope runs through the noseband. This will prevent the halter from becoming either too tight or too loose.

When you reach the stable, or the place where you are planning to groom and saddle up your pony, tie him up securely with a quick-release knot of the type which will not become difficult to undo if he pulls backwards for any reason. It is wise to loop a piece of string through the ring you are tying him to and then tie the rope to the string. If he does run back he will break the string and not the headcollar or halter.

Having caught and tied up your pony you will need to groom him before he is ready for your ride, but remember that when the time comes for you to turn him out again never let him gallop off the moment you get through the gate into the field. Turn him round to face the gate, give him a pat and then let him go free.

Above: the correct way to approach a pony.

Left: putting on a headcollar.

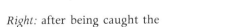

Right: after being caught the pony is led away.

5
Principles of correct feeding

HORSES HAVE SMALL STOMACHS for their size and when they are allowed to roam freely they graze almost continuously so that their stomachs receive small quantities of food on a regular basis. They will also drink at frequent intervals small amounts of water in between grazing.

A stabled horse, however, is normally fed several relatively large meals which will take longer to digest. If he drinks a lot of water soon after he has fed, because his stomach is so small, the food will be washed out into his intestine before it is really ready for the next stage of its digestive process. This can cause colic and other gastric troubles.

It is wise to make sure that a horse always has a plentiful supply of water in his stable. He can then drink whenever he wants to in the same way as he would if he were in his natural state. If a supply is not to hand, always water a horse before feeding – and do *not* water him again for at least two hours.

All horses need roughage, and the best basic food for a stabled horse is hay which also helps to provide the bulk needed to fill his rather large frame. The best is seed hay, harvested early in summer before the seed and leaf have fallen. Hay made later may look equally good but it will lack the essential seed value and vitamins.

Good hay is greenish or light brown in colour, but not yellow. It should be crisp and sweet to the taste and have a fragrant aroma. Cheap, poor-quality hay which is dusty and has a musty smell will turn out to be the most expensive in the long run. Horses and ponies cannot cope with dust, and all sorts of digestive and respiratory troubles can result from bad hay.

The amount of hay given depends on many factors and we illustrate on the next page some of the recommended amounts. New forms of bulk feed are becoming increasingly available, and where this is given care should be taken to see that the manufacturer's instructions are followed. Whatever feed is given a close watch on the condition of the horse or pony is necessary to ensure he is not losing condition.

Assuming a horse is stabled, clipped-out and rugged, and is in work, the following example shows the feed which might be given each day:

	14.2hh	15.2hh	16.2hh
Hay	4.5–5.4kg	5.5kg	6kg
Chaff or bran	1.0–1.3kg	1.0–1.8kg	1.0–1.8kg
Oats or barley	2.7kg	4.5–5.4kg	5.4–6.0kg

For a child's pony, say between 12.2hh and 13.2hh the recommended daily feed is:

	During summer months and kept at grass	During winter months when stabled at night and at grass during the day
Hay	none	2.3–2.7kg
Bran	0.2–0.5kg	0.2–0.5kg
Pony nuts/cubes	1.8kg	1.8kg

Pony cubes or nuts may be used instead of oats, but always be sure to follow the manufacturer's recommended rate.

Some owners allow their horses as much hay as they will eat, making it available at all times. Provided the hay is of good quality, and the animal does not become too fat, this is quite a sound practice. But the nature and amount of feed must be carefully adjusted to take into account the points made in the following pages.

Horses in gentle work – those perhaps only asked to exert themselves at weekends – can do quite well on hay supplemented with small feeds of corn mixed with bran and chaff (finely chopped hay and straw), preferably fed dampened. Chaff can be mixed with molasses to give it flavour.

If you want a horse to do any strenuous work, however, you

will have to provide him with more protein. A horse which you are trying to get really hard and fit will need plenty of muscle-building food such as oats and barley. Some brands of good quality nuts are also rich in proteins, but it is as well to find out exactly what the nuts contain before feeding them.

Even if a horse is out at grass and you only want to use him at weekends, you will have to augment his grazing with hay and some protein feeds. It is much wiser to give him small feeds each day than to give him large feeds at the weekend – when he is expected to work.

Always remember that ponies out at grass require plenty of good quality hay in the winter when there is little or no nutritious value in the grazing. They must also have a constant supply of fresh water all the year round.

Careful feeding is essential for stabled horses and ponies and a balanced diet found for their temperaments and needs.

The best food for working horses is **oats** which should be short, plump and shiny with thin husks. They should always have a pleasant taste and smell, and weigh quite heavy in the hand. If you put some in your palm and grip the husks tightly they should

Above: this illustration shows some of the many different foodstuffs in regular use for horses and ponies.

Above: it is a sound practice, before giving a haynet, to soak the hay with water. This removes any dust and makes the hay more easily digested.

spring apart, leaving a slight trace of flour when you open your hand. On no account feed oats which are dusty or which smell musty. Some people prefer feeding oats which have been crushed or bruised, but others like to feed the grains whole.

Bran is of little real food value, being the residue from milled wheat. It does, however, add bulk to a feed, and is good for the digestion because it makes the animal masticate his food. It should be dry, sweet and flaky. The broader variety is the best. The illustrations on pages 44–45 show how to make a bran mash.

Barley is particularly useful as an alternative to oats, especially for ponies who may become rather too frisky when they are fed oats. It is also good for young animals, being an excellent bone builder. Because the husks are very hard, barley must *always* be crushed or boiled before being fed. The grains should be plump, short and hard. They must also be pale gold in colour and quite odourless.

Although oats, bran, barley and chaff can make up the main ingredients for a healthy diet, there are other alternatives which may be fed either to supplement the feed or make it more tempting.

Root crops, such as carrots, mangolds, swedes, turnips or even potatoes, are pleasant to feed, but they have little real food value. They must, however, always be sliced lengthways before being fed, otherwise they may become stuck in a horse's gullet. Raw potatoes make a good supplementary feed for horses or ponies who are gone in the wind.

Flake maize mixed with oats also makes a pleasant change of diet, though it is inclined to be fattening. **Sugar-beet pulp** has quite a lot of food value, but it must be soaked for at least 24 hours before being fed. **Linseed**, which is the seed of the flax plant, is an extremely useful addition to the fodder store, because it can be used in a variety of ways – including as linseed jelly, tea, gruel or mash. It must always be ground, boiled or soaked beforehand. Being rich in protein and fat, it should be used sparingly. It is useful as a tonic or when you want to improve the look of your horse's coat.

Making a bran mash.

Above, top: add a little salt to the bran.

Below: pour in boiling water with great care.

The concentrates provided in **horse and pony cubes** or **nuts** can save on time and labour because they provide a ready mixed diet. It is important to be absolutely sure that you know exactly what proteins you are feeding, however, and in what quantities. Some horses and ponies react differently to the various brands and mixtures of nuts, so feeding concentrates in this form is a matter of trial and error. Like the **vitamins** on sale for mixing with the feeds, they need to be used sensibly and not looked upon as being a lazy short cut to proper feeding.

All foodstuff should be kept in rat-proof and damp-proof bins. If you do get vermin in your fodder store, do not put down poison but use a trap, or better still, get a good stable-cat. Poison can get on to the feet of vermin and become mixed with the feed. It is also important to remember that domestic pets, such as cats and dogs, can become poisoned themselves if they eat or even bite a rat or mouse that has eaten poison.

When planning a stable timetable, the basic rule must always be to feed little and often, and to restrict each feed to no more than 1.8kg (4lb), because the horse's stomach is not large enough to cope properly with bigger amounts. Try and vary the diet as much as possible. After all, no one likes eating the same thing meal after meal, day after day!

Successful dieting is a matter of finding out what is best for a horse or pony so that he remains fit and happy without becoming either too fat or too much of a handful.

Try and give a horse a regular day off each week. On the

Above, top: stir well.

Below: place a sack over the bucket and allow mash to cool before feeding.

evening before his rest day, when he should only have light walking exercise, give him a light laxative in the form of a bran mash. His regular feeds must be drastically reduced on his day off or he may become a victim of what is known as azoturia, or 'Monday morning disease'. It was given that name years ago by the grooms looking after working horses which had been rested on Sunday without having had their regular feeds reduced sufficiently to take into account the fact that they would not be getting their usual exercise on that day. Azoturia is a very unpleasant illness which affects the muscles and can prove fatal.

The nine points to always remember when considering good feeding practice are:

1. Feed little and often
2. Wherever possible allow a stable-kept horse some grazing each day
3. Ensure each horse or pony is given sufficient bulk food, such as hay
4. Try always to feed at the same time each day
5. Never introduce sudden changes to the type of food being given. Where change is necessary be sure to introduce it gradually
6. Take extra care to see that only good, clean foreage is given
7. Never ask a horse or pony to undertake exercise or work immediately following a feed
8. Give water before feeding, and be sure there is always a supply of fresh water available in the stable or field
9. Feed according to the amount of work being done, but take into account the type and age of the horse or pony, its condition and fitness, the time of year, the nutritious value of the grazing

A linseed mash is useful for putting some flesh on to a horse if he is in poor condition. Boil about 0.5kg (1lb) of linseed slowly for about three hours until all the grains become soft. The water left should be enough to soak up 0.5kg (1lb) of bran. Add the bran paste to the cooked linseed and stir them both together into a thick paste which will then be ready to feed.

Linseed jelly is an excellent tonic which can be added to normal feeds. The linseed needs to be cooked very slowly for several hours. It will have to be stirred regularly, to prevent it from becoming stuck to the side of the container, until it turns into a jelly with a texture rather like that of household starch. Drain away the water which can then be used as another good tonic –

linseed tea. If you prefer to soak the linseed in water for about twenty-four hours it will also jellify. Decide which is the most convenient method. **Linseed gruel** is excellent for a tired horse. Cook the linseed in the way you would for a linseed mash, then strain it through a muslin to get rid of all the grain. You should feed it to a horse or pony immediately it is cool enough – before it turns to jelly.

The Combined System
The combined system of keeping is the routine by which a stable-kept horse or pony spends part of each day at grass. This must never be considered an alternative method, but one which is a compromise between a stable-kept horse and one which is kept at grass – both having been dealt with in the previous pages.

The combined system works well for riders who do not wish to compete seriously and not expect their horses to undertake strenuous work. The best method is to stable the horse by day during summer months and by night during the winter, allowing him to spend the rest of the time in the field. The animal will then require attention only in the morning or evening.

Provided that the field has an adequate shelter, preferably one that can be adapted to enable the horse to be kept in when required, the combined system works extremely well and has many advantages.

During the winter months the horse or pony will be clean and dry and be ready to be ridden in the morning. Conversely, in the summer, he will be in a condition to be ridden in the evening when it is cool. A horse kept by this system can be trace-clipped in winter, provided he is turned out in a New Zealand rug and is properly rugged up at night. He will also be kept fitter than a fully grass-kept horse since his grass intake will be restricted, thereby making him less likely to suffer from laminitis and other problems associated with overweight horses.

If you do decide to change a horse or pony's diet you must do so gradually, otherwise he may develop colic – an illness of the digestive system sometimes referred to as 'gripes'. It can also be caused by poor quality food or too much cold water given when a horse is hot.

The signs are: the animal will be in obvious pain, trying to kick at his belly, and looking round at his flanks. He will also want to lie down and roll. You should call the veterinary surgeon if the symptoms continue and, while you are waiting for him to arrive, keep the animal warm and walk him around. The veterinary surgeon will probably recommend a draught made up with an opiate.

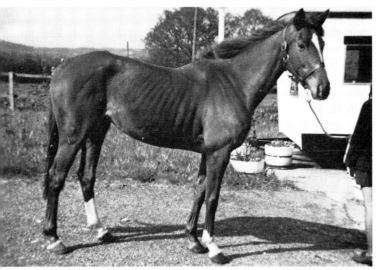

The importance of worming and proper feeding.

Left: this Thoroughbred mare badly needed worming and had not been fed correctly.

Right: three weeks after being wormed and given the correct diet and careful exercise she began to improve.

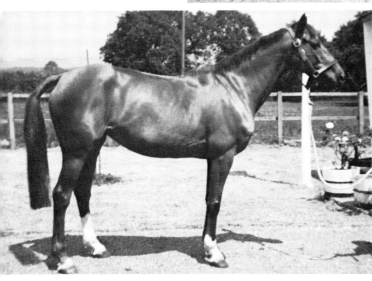

Left: after six weeks the mare showed her quality and was ready to go into training.

6
Grooming

Although grooming improves the appearance of a pony, there are more important reasons than this for a regular grooming routine. The skin is as vital to a pony's health as either his lungs or his heart, and grooming not only promotes health, it also helps maintain condition, prevents disease and ensures cleanliness.

When a pony is turned out during the winter months he grows a long coat which is very difficult to keep clean, and the grease and scurf in the coat help to keep him warm and make the hair more waterproof.

When the weather is cold and wet, grooming should be restricted to a good going-over with a dandy brush or a rubber curry comb to remove the worst of the mud. The pony's feet should, of course, be picked out each day with a hoof pick, and the mane and tail kept tidy with a body brush. The pony's eyes, muzzle and dock will also need sponging with clean water, but that is really all that can or should be done in the winter months if the pony is out.

In the summer – or if the pony is stabled – he will need a thorough grooming to help keep him fit and well. Always groom to a system. In that way you will be less likely to forget anything.

Your grooming kit should be kept in a special box or basket, or a big canvas bag. Put all the items of grooming kit away carefully when you finish working. They will then be ready for you when you next need them, and all you will have to find is a bucket of clean water. Never leave brushes lying on the ground. They will only get dirty, and you will not get a clean pony with a dirty brush.

Begin by taking the hoof pick, which will enable you to remove any stones or dirt which may have become lodged between the shoe and the frog – the V-shaped cleft in the centre of the foot. Picking up each foot in turn, work downwards with the hoof pick from the heel towards the toe. Clear the cleft of the frog and look for any signs of thrush (an inflammatory condition noticeable mainly by a discharge and a foul smell). How to deal with foot ailments like thrush is dealt with in chapter 14.

Next, tap the shoe firmly with the handle of the hoof pick to

Right: grooming kit.

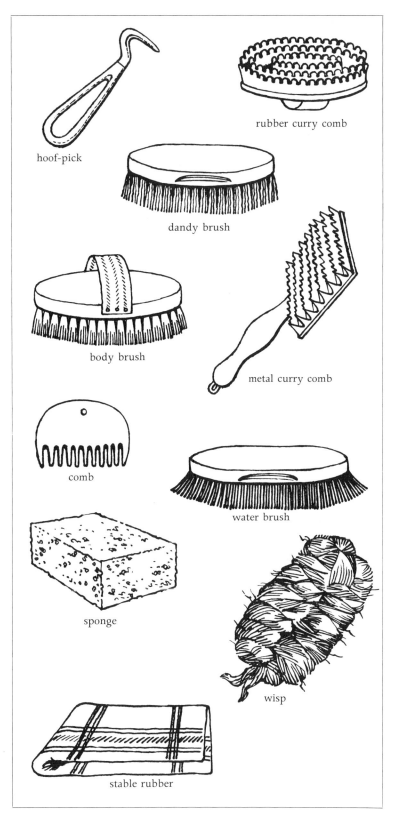

hoof-pick

rubber curry comb

dandy brush

body brush

metal curry comb

comb

water brush

sponge

wisp

stable rubber

Left: grooming must always begin with the feet being 'picked-out'. By correctly using a hoof pick you remove any stones or dirt which has become lodged between the shoe and frog. Horses and ponies, whether stable-kept or grass-kept, should have their feet dealt with every day.

Getting to work with the dandy brush

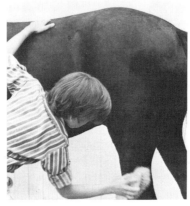

. . . not forgetting the legs

the body brush being used on the mane

. . . and getting dust out of the coat

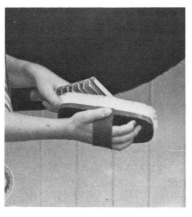

the brush needs to be scraped clean

. . . and the curry comb tapped clean on the floor

Above: checking the pony's feet for any sign of risen clenches

make sure that is secure. Finally run your fingers round the side of the hoof to see that all the nails are smooth, and none are sticking out to form risen clenches.

Because tidiness is important, it is a good idea to clean out the dirt and stones from the pony's hooves into a dung skip – a round container or basket used for picking out droppings in the stable.

The really energetic part of the grooming now begins. Take the dandy brush – a wooden-backed brush with strong bristles – and remove all the caked mud and sweat marks. Start at the top of the neck and, using the brush in a to-and-fro movement, pay particular attention to parts of the body such as the saddle region, the belly, and the points of the hocks and the fetlocks.

Change the brush over from one hand to the other and, if there is a lot of mud and the hair is long, you may find it easier to use a rubber curry comb in a circular motion.

When all the mud has been removed, exchange the dandy

the headcollar must be looped around the neck

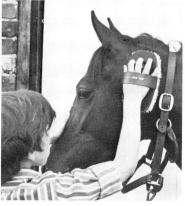

. . . before carefully brushing the pony's head

the wisp will help tone-up the pony

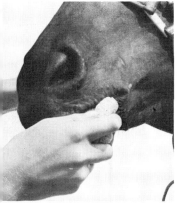

a damp sponge is used for the eyes, nose and mouth

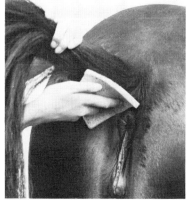

and another for the dock area

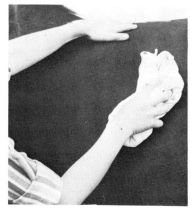

the stable rubber removes any last traces of dust

brush for the body brush. This is an oval-shaped brush of short, closely set bristles, with a thick band of webbing fixed to the sides to help you to hold it firmly.

Although the main purpose of the body brush is to remove dust and sweat from the body, neck and quarters, it is also used to keep the mane and tail tidy.

As you should always start at the front of a pony, begin with the mane by pushing it across to the wrong side of the neck and thoroughly brush the crest. Then, letting the mane fall back into its correct position, start at the withers, separating a few locks of hair at a time, and carefully brush out any tangles. Work slowly along the neck, only trying to deal with a few locks of hair at a time.

When you start removing the dust from a pony's coat the body brush will quickly become clogged unless you use a curry comb. This has a wooden handle and the comb is scraped across the body brush to remove the dust.

Take the body brush in one hand and the curry comb in the other and, standing by the pony's neck on the near side, brush the coat in short circular strokes in the direction of the hair.

As you are doing this, stand well back from the pony and lean the weight of your body behind the brush, working with a slightly bent arm and supple wrist. After every few strokes remove the dirt from the body brush by drawing it smartly across the teeth of the curry comb, and then tapping the comb on the floor, behind the pony, and not on the stable wall.

After the near side has been finished, change over, and, using the curry comb and body brush, groom the pony's off side.

When his body and legs have been brushed thoroughly, move round to his head and slip off the headcollar. You can still keep him tied safely by buckling the headstrap loosely round his neck.

Ponies are usually quite happy to have their heads groomed gently, but they will resist any rough treatment. The curry comb will not be needed when you are brushing a pony's head. Thus with one hand you can hold him still and, holding the brush in the other, work away quietly, trying to avoid any tender areas or bony projections. When you have finished, the headcollar can be replaced, and the body brush given a final clean on the curry comb.

The only part left to do now will be the tail. In the same way as you did the mane, tackle only a few locks of hair at a time and brush out the tangles. The easiest way is to hold the tail in one hand and shake out a few hairs at a time with your fingers. Use the body brush on the tail and never the dandy brush, which will only tend to remove or break the hairs.

It is not time, however, for you to stand back and admire the

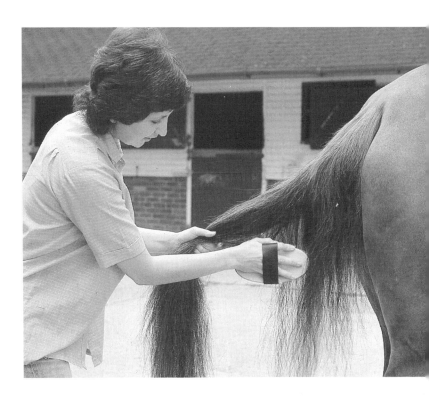

results, because your pony still needs a massage to help harden up his muscles. A massage will also improve his blood supply and produce a shine on his coat by squeezing oil from the glands of his skin. This body massage can either be done with a wisp – a tightly-woven rope of twisted hay or straw – or with a special leather pad.

The wisp should be dampened slightly with water and used vigorously by bringing it down with a bang in the direction of the lay of the coat. Pay special attention to those parts where the muscles are hard and flat – such as the sides of the neck, the quarters and thighs – but take care to avoid the tender region of the loins and any bony prominences. As you bring the wisp down in a steady rhythmic movement you should be able to see the muscles twitch. Most of the really hard work is now over, but you have not finished yet.

Wring out the sponge in a bucket of clean water to make sure that it is soft, clean and damp. Then, holding your pony's head still, gently sponge his eyes – moving away from the corners and around the eyelids. Clean the sponge and wipe the muzzle region – including the lips and the inside and outside of the nostrils.

Wring out a second sponge and, lifting the pony's tail as high as you can, clean the whole of the dock area, including the skin underneath the tail. This is most important because sponging helps to refresh a pony. He will probably appreciate this more than any other part of the grooming routine.

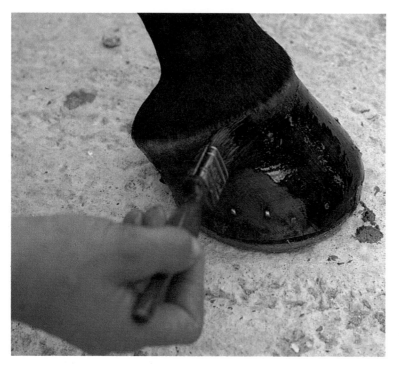

Left: adding hoof oil is part of the grooming process. Oil does more than improve appearance of the feet – it helps to prevent them from becoming brittle and cracked.

While you have the water bucket handy 'lay' the mane by dipping the end hairs of the water brush in the bucket and, after shaking away the excess water, lay the hair flat by brushing it from the roots downwards.

Unless the weather is extremely cold and frosty, the water brush can also be used to wash a pony's feet. If you do wash his hooves, it is important to keep the thumb of the hand holding the pony's foot pressed well into the hollow of the heel to prevent water from becoming lodged there.

When the hooves are dry they will be ready to be oiled. A small brush dipped in a jar of hoof oil is the best way of doing this. Oil will not only improve the appearance but also help prevent brittle or broken feet.

Finally, take a slightly dampened stable rubber and go all over the pony's coat to remove the last traces of dust.

Allow plenty of time for grooming. An experienced groom will usually take about thirty minutes, but remember that if it is going to be effective it must be done thoroughly each day.

There are electrically operated grooming machines, which are especially useful in stables where there are a number of horses to do and when labour is short. They have a massaging effect, and are quite efficient at removing dirt and grease as well as putting a final polish to the coat. The tail, however, should be tied out of the way, and you should wear a hat or headscarf, for the sake of safety, if your hair is long.

7
Saddlery and equipment

WHEN ANYONE MENTIONS SADDLERY you will probably immediately visualise the saddles and bridles, girths, stirrups and leathers in use every day. People rarely stop to think of the wide variety of bits, martingales and other equipment which are available to riders to help make their horses and ponies more comfortable to ride and, in addition, easier to control.

A well-fitting saddle and bridle are essential if you expect a horse or pony to be comfortable and at the same time be in the right frame of mind to carry out your wishes without resistance. No horse can be expected to give of his best while being subjected to saddlery which is either ill-fitting or unsuitable for his particular action or temperament. The first thing you must do is to check your saddlery and make sure it fits and is of the correct type.

Saddles
A badly fitting saddle will cause discomfort to both you and the horse or pony and can seriously hamper his movements. Horses, like humans, may look similar in build, but they are never completely identical in shape or character, and for this reason it is best for every horse to have his own saddle which can be allowed to settle down and mould to the shape of his back.

The term 'all purpose' or 'general purpose' which are given to saddles means that they are suitable for a variety of uses – such as hacking, hunting or jumping. It does not mean that one saddle will fit every type of horse. Quite the opposite is often the case and, if you do use the same saddle on different horses, it will eventually not fit any of them correctly, and the horses will almost certainly end up with sore backs.

A good horse or pony deserves a good saddle. There is after all little sense in spending time, money and effort in schooling him properly, and getting him fit and well, if you are going to spoil everything by not providing him with a saddle which will be comfortable for you both.

Quite apart from your own comfort – and making sure that the saddle in no way retards your horse's freedom of movement –

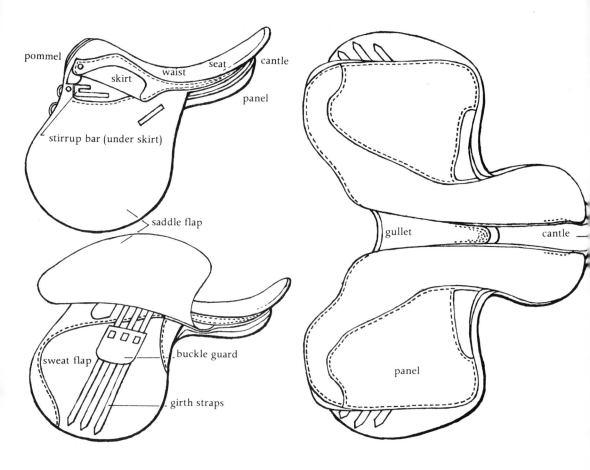

pommel · skirt · waist · seat · cantle · panel · stirrup bar (under skirt) · saddle flap · sweat flap · buckle guard · girth straps · gullet · cantle · panel

remember that pressure and friction are the two most frequent causes of soreness and must be avoided at all costs. The first essential is to see that the tree – the framework on which the saddle is constructed – fits correctly. The tree is usually made in three sizes – narrow, medium and broad. Take a look at the diagram of the saddle and you will see the names given to the various parts.

Although a good saddler can sometimes make a narrow tree broader, he cannot successfully make a broad tree narrower. At least his efforts will not prove to be successful in the long run, and so it is not really worth trying. Attempting to put stuffing into the front of a saddle with too broad a tree will only tend to throw the saddle out of balance, and taking stuffing out of a narrow saddle to try to make it fit a broader animal will be equally ineffective. If the saddle is too narrow the points of the tree will pinch and cause soreness, and if it is too wide, the arch will bear down on the withers and again cause discomfort. Modern trees allow for quite a lot of flexibility in fitting, and if the saddle also happens to have a sloped back head, it can probably be made to fit quite a number

Above: this illustration shows the names given to the various parts of a saddle. It is important that, like the 'points of the horse', the names are studied and remembered. They are used on many occasions.

of horses. However, once the right fit has been achieved, it is best to stick to the rule of one saddle, one horse.

It is wise to get the advice of a competent saddler if you are not sure whether a saddle really fits because getting it right can save a lot of problems later on. When you have checked that the tree is the correct size, the next task is to see that the saddle gives complete clearance of the withers and along the backbone. Sit in the saddle and check whether you can put three fingers between the front arch of the saddle and the horse's withers. If you cannot, there will not be enough clearance for comfort.

While you are still in the saddle get someone to check that the underneath panels bear evenly on either side of the animal's back, also that the channel between the panels is deep enough and wide enough to be clear of the backbone at all paces and when you are jumping. It is important, however, while noting that there is not undue pressure in the wrong places, to check that the saddle still fits snugly and is as close to the horse's back as possible.

Saddles need re-stuffing at regular intervals because the weight of the rider will in time make the panels flat, so that there is not enough clearance in the channel. To prevent this from happening, take the saddle to a good saddler. He will be able to re-shape it.

Badly fitting saddles are, of course, not the only cause of sore backs. Stable rollers with pads so flat that they are bound to put constant pressure on a horse's spine, and are then done up too tightly, can cause a considerable amount of trouble. Putting some sacking or a rubber pad under the roller is not the real answer. It is essential that a horse's backbone should be free of pressure at all times, and so the roller should be stuffed and fitted in the same way as you would for a saddle.

Saddles which are too long in the tree put too much pressure on the loins and, apart from soreness, may also cause irreparable damage to the horse's kidneys. If a large rider sits in a saddle which is too small, his weight will be concentrated over too restricted an area of the horse's back and cause similar problems.

In the case of a fat pony kept out at grass – where it is more difficult to keep him to a diet – you may be faced with the problem of a saddle which continually rides forwards over the withers, making it not only uncomfortable for the pony, but also very disconcerting for the rider. The only real solution is a crupper which will go under the pony's tail and fasten on to the back of the saddle.

The crupper can be adjusted according to the saddle and the size of the pony. A serge-lined saddle, instead of a leather-lined one can also sometimes be of help. Numnahs and wither pads should never be regarded as a permanent solution to an ill-fitting saddle.

Left: making a saddle demands a high degree of skill. This traditional craft is one of the oldest known. *Below:* saddles of one sort or another have been in use for thousands of years.

Right: the Western saddle, now being more widely used throughout the world, originated in the United States. Note the intricate and delicate design and tooling. Also to be seen is the different pommel to that found on an all-purpose saddle (see below).

Above: an all-purpose or general-purpose saddle is shown here with a girth and with the stirrups having been 'run up'. This saddle rests on a specially-constructed saddle horse.

Some riders like using a numnah because they feel it acts as an additional cushion between the saddle and the horse's back. Others, however, are of the opinion that a numnah quickly becomes saturated with sweat, and can cause overheating, leading to a sore back. Providing a saddle fits well and the panels are maintained properly, there seems little reason for a numnah which will, if anything, place a rider further away from his horse and not give him the correct feel. If you do use a numnah, however, the best is probably the type made of plastic foam which does not cause heating of the back, and is relatively easy to keep clean.

Wither pads are more usual in racing circles, although they can be used as a temporary measure if a saddle has begun to sink in the front.

If you need a new saddle, and it is difficult for your saddler to come and see your horse or pony, there is a useful way of measuring a horse's back. You will need a thick piece of lead – or a thick piece of wire – about 46cm (18in) long. This should be shaped over the withers of the horse at about the place where you would expect the front or head of the saddle to be. Press the wire

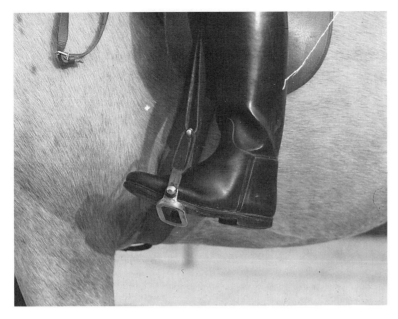

Left: a form of safety stirrup which enables the foot to be quickly released should an accident happen.

down until it forms the shape of the back, and then transfer it to a piece of paper so that the outline can be traced. Repeat the process, only this time take the measurement back about 25cm (10in) from the first measurement, and then to complete the job take a final measurement along the length of the back from the withers. If you add to this details of your own height, weight, and inside leg measurement to the knee, your local saddler will have quite a lot of information to go on in suggesting a suitable saddle.

There are a number of different types for you to choose from, depending on what you want to do. A general purpose saddle will have a wide variety of uses, or you may require a show saddle, a hunting saddle, a dressage saddle (with its straight front), or a jumping saddle (with its forward cut). A child's saddle can vary from a felt pad to a smaller version of the general purpose saddle. Some have full panels and others have short panels, which are meant to allow the small rider to have a better 'feel' and grip.

Every saddle needs a good sound girth to hold it in place. These vary in size from about 92cm (36in) for a small pony to 1.35m (54in) for a large horse. They are made of leather, webbing, lampwick, or nylon cord. The most expensive, but undoubtedly the best, are those made of leather, providing that they are properly looked after and kept supple.

Leathers

Stirrup leathers are made of either cowhide, rawhide or buffalo hide. All leathers stretch, and rawhide and buffalo hide will frequently stretch more than cowhide. As riders usually place

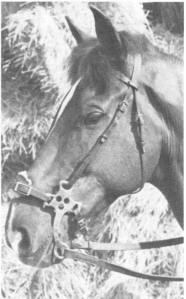

Right: a Kimblewick shown with a 'Flash' noseband and standing martingale. The throat lash here needs tightening a hole or two.

Far right: a Hackamore.

more weight in one stirrup iron than the other, especially when mounting, the leathers ought to be changed over at regular intervals to ensure that one does not become more stretched than the other. Because all new leathers will stretch they should never be worn for competitions or hunting until they have had time to settle down.

Stirrup irons
Stirrup irons should preferably be made from stainless steel, and they must always be large enough to let boots go in and out without hindrance. A good, heavy stirrup iron will also free the foot more easily in the event of a fall.

Bridles
There are five main types of bridle. Apart from the snaffle – which is the most common of all – there is the Pelham, the Weymouth, the gag and the bitless bridle. Although bridles may have different bits, they all have a headpiece which includes the throatlash to prevent the bridle from slipping over the horse's head; cheek pieces which buckle on to either side of the headpiece (and to which the bit is secured); the browband which helps to hold the headpiece in place; the cavesson or noseband to which a standing martingale can be attached, and the reins.

In a double bridle the bridoon or snaffle bit is secured by a secondary strap and cheekpiece, which passes through the slots of the browband. The double bridle and the Pelham both have two pairs of reins and a lipstrap which passes through a ring on the curb chain and keeps it in place in the curb groove.

Nosebands

A plain cavesson is always used with a double bridle, but there are various other nosebands, such as the elegantly stitched ones used mostly for showing, the sheepskin-covered nosebands – originally used in the United States of America to prevent trotting horses from shying, but which are now popular among racehorse trainers – and the drop noseband which is fastened round the muzzle below a snaffle bit in order to prevent a horse from pulling and also to ensure that he cannot open his mouth far enough to hand out his tongue.

There is also a 'flash' noseband – an ordinary cavesson noseband with two diagonal crossing straps sewn on to the centre which also are fastened beneath the bit. It is used instead of an ordinary drop noseband when a standing martingale is required.

Above: the Drop noseband, with the fastening below the snaffle bit. This is a much used modern bitting arrangement, and one recommended for younger riders.

Right: one of the several variations of the basic Drop noseband is the Flash, with its cross-over or figure of eight design.

Reins

The reins can be made of leather, webbing, plaited nylon or plaited cotton, although leather reins are sometimes covered in rubber to give a better grip when hunting or show jumping. The rubber covering should be stitched by hand with a large spot stitch down the centre. In time, the rubber will wear smooth and need to be replaced by the saddler. Webbing reins also provide a good grip in wet weather, but whereas the soft plaited cotton reins are excellent in most conditions, plaited nylon reins are inclined to stretch and slip.

The normal length of a full size rein is about 1.5m (5ft) but reins used on children's ponies are usually much shorter or they would be inclined to hang down in a loop which could catch the rider's feet.

Far left: a Pelham, used with a Cavesson noseband. The throat lash appears to need loosening a hole or two.

Left: a Double bridle.

Bits

Bits help to impose control on a horse by putting pressure on the corners and bars of the mouth, the tongue, the poll, the nose, the roof of the mouth and with some bits, the curb groove. The object of a bit is to assist the rider to position his horse's head to give maximum control over speed and direction. Various bits act in various ways, and there is a wide variety from which to choose – ranging from the plain jointed snaffle to the double bridle, with its two bits and double reins.

A double bridle should never be used by an inexpert rider. In the wrong hands it can cause a horse both discomfort and possible harm. It has a bridoon or snaffle bit, below which is fitted the curb bit with its curb chain and lip strap. The bridoon is usually jointed and the curb has a straight bar mouthpiece with an upward bend in the middle, known as the port. A double bridle achieves the correct positioning of the horse's head by raising it with the snaffle bit, and lowering it and bringing the nose inwards by means of the curb. In Britain the bridoon rein is usually held on the outside of the rider's little finger – outside the curb rein to emphasise the action of the bridoon – but in France the bridoon rein is held between the third and fourth fingers, and the curb rein under the little finger – which puts more emphasis on the curb bit. In this way, the reins correspond to the position of the bridoon and the curb bit in the animal's mouth.

The Pelham is a cross between a snaffle and a double bridle. It uses two reins, but the mouthpiece is a mullen or halfmoon-shaped one of either metal or vulcanite and is fitted with a curb

Above: a 'Grackle' noseband needs to be carefully fitted.

Right: the Kimblewick, a most popular bit used by yonger riders, is a form of Pelham. This has a straight bit, with a small port, short cheekpieces and a curb chain, all controlled by a single rein.

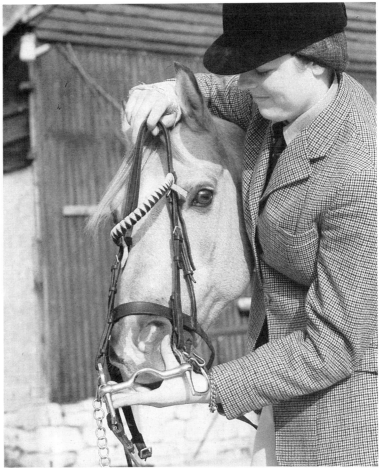

chain. Children sometimes use a Pelham with leather roundings which join the snaffle and curb rings so that a single rein can be used.

In many countries the Kimblewick is an even more popular bit for young riders because it is really a form of Pelham with a straight bit, having a small port, short cheekpieces, and a curb chain, but using a single rein.

The gag is an exaggerated snaffle, with the rings having holes in the top and bottom through which goes a cheekpiece of rounded leather with the reins attached. It is particularly helpful on horses when jumping who approach their fences too quickly, with their heads held low.

If you want to check the size of a bit, remember that snaffle bits are measured between the rings when laid flat. A mullen mouthpiece is also measured between the rings.

Most varieties of bitless bridle including the best known of these, the Hackamore, combine pressure on the nose with pressure on the curb groove, and they have cheekpieces which

Left: a running martingale, one of the artificial 'aids' helps to lower a horse's head. This is fastened at one end to the girth, with rings at the other end through which the reins pass.

are sufficiently long to give the rider considerable leverage. They are extremely useful for a horse or pony whose mouth has been so damaged that he will not go well in any other type of bridle, but Hackamores and bitless bridles are not permitted in pony competitions only when jumping under the Rules of the British Show Jumping Association.

Martingales

Martingales are sometimes needed to help lower a horse's head. They give the rider more control by preventing any evasion of the bit, and are frequently used in jumping – if a horse's head can be held low the neck can still be stretched he will jump with a round, supple back and be less likely to hit a fence than he would if he flung up his head and hollowed his back. If the martingale is too tight, however, the horse will not have enough freedom to extend his neck outwards and downwards when he is jumping. His ability to jump spread fences will then be seriously impaired.

There are four main types of martingale. First there is the standing martingale, which has a loop at either end; one fastens on to the girth between the forelegs and the other on to the noseband. Like all but one of the martingales, it has a neck strap to keep it in position. Then there is the running martingale which again fastens on to the girth, but the other end divides into two straps with rings for the reins to pass through. If a running martingale is used with a double bridle, the bridoon or snaffle rein is passed through the rings. These are the only two martingales permitted in show jumping competitions.

The bib martingale is rather like the running martingale, but has a triangular piece of leather sewn between the branches holding the rings to prevent an excited horse from getting himself tangled up. The last of the four main types of martingale, the Irish rings, look rather like a pair of spectacles, and is sometimes called an Irish martingale. The rings do not affect the position of the horse's head, but they prevent the reins from going over his head – particularly during a fall.

Taking care of tack

Saddlery must always be well looked after. It is expensive and should be made to last. It must also be kept in good order from the point of view of safety.

Broken stitching or brittle leather straps can prove a menace. It is up to the rider to make sure that his or her equipment is both checked and cleaned properly and regularly. Cleaning tack need not be a chore. If the weather is fine it can be done outside – the task will then seem much more enjoyable.

Water, heat and neglect are the three things which will ruin

Below: all tack requires regular cleaning and, when the weather is bright, this is a job which can be tackled outdoors. Cleaning tack also gives an opportunity to check for wear or for damaged stitching.

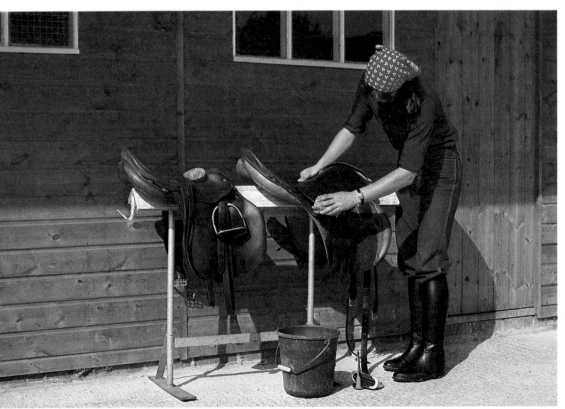

leather more quickly than anything else. Leather loses a percentage of its fat content every day – and the heat and sweat from a horse's body will quickly help to make it dry and brittle and ready to crack.

Saddles, bridles and other items of leather equipment should be cleaned with a damp sponge after every use and then finished off with saddle soap which should be applied with a slightly damp sponge. About once a week go over all the leather with one of the preparations on the market for keeping leather supple, but be careful not to overfeed the leather otherwise you will make it flabby and greasy. Do not put too much grease on the outside of your saddle, because it will not be absorbed and will only dirty your breeches. Always take a bridle to pieces to clean it, and undo all the buckles on stirrup leathers and martingales.

Bits, stirrup irons and curb chains will need washing in warm soapy water, and then they should be given a good polish with a dry cloth.

Stable equipment

Apart from the saddlery needed for riding your horse, you will also have to think about equipment for the stable. A good stable headcollar is the first essential. Try not to buy a cheap one with galvanised or tinned buckles, because a brass-mounted headcollar, with a rolled leather throat strap – and at least two rows of stitching on the cheeks and back stay – will always look smarter and, in addition, will last longer. If you have a small pony a Dutch slip or even a yearling headcollar, which is adjustable, will sometimes do quite well. Whatever type of leather headcollar you use, however, do not forget that it will need cleaning.

It is also useful to have a pad for protecting your horse's poll when he is travelling. This is a felt pad with slots through which the head strap of the headcollar can be passed to hold it in place, but the headcollar must have a browband to prevent the pad from sliding over the horse's head.

You will also need a stout rope fitted with a safety hook to clip on to the metal square at the head of the headcollar when the horse is tied up or being led, although some prefer to use rack chains in the stable. If your horse is inclined to run backwards when he is tied up, you will have problems with broken headcollars. The immediate answer – until you can cure him of the habit – will be a strong rope halter, preferably of the type which has a throatlash to stop it from getting pulled over the ears.

Water buckets, hay nets and a feed bowl of the larger metal variety which cannot be knocked over are also needed in a stable. Large plastic or rubber buckets which are easy to keep clean are quite adequate. They do not become slimy like wooden buckets, and are less heavy, and they do not rattle like metal ones if they get kicked or knocked over. Hay nets are invaluable because – apart from enabling hay to be weighed before being fed – they also prevent waste, as the animal can pick out a mouthful at a time. This discourages him from eating too quickly, and the hay does not get trodden into the bedding or kicked around the box as it would do if it were fed on the floor.

You must make sure you hang the net up high enough to keep it out of the way of the pony's legs when it becomes empty but not so high that seeds can fall into his eyes. To ensure the former, pull the neck cord tight when the net has been filled and pull the loop through the hay-net ring on the stable wall until it is the correct height. Then thread the end of the loop through two or three of the strands of cord near the bottom of the hay net and pull it upwards until you can tie it through the ring with a quick release knot. In this way the hay net will be tied up double and will not hang low when empty.

Hay nets made of tarred cord are meant to prevent a horse from chewing the netting. This is usually rather a forlorn hope, but if you have to dampen down your horse's hay the tar does help prevent the cord from rotting too quickly. Of course, all nets will rot in time if they are constantly subjected to water.

When feeding hay in a field use a hay rack to prevent waste.

Another important stable item is a skip for removing droppings. The basket types are light and easy to use, and a deep one is particularly handy. There are also some plastic and rubber muck skips which are quite satisfactory.

Rugs

When you start buying rugs you will have to decide exactly what you want because, apart from being expensive, they take up a considerable amount of room and need regular attention if they are not to become both worn and torn.

The most important rug – if a horse is stabled – is without doubt a night or stable rug, usually made from jute and lined with blanketing. There are, however, some other types of proprietary night rugs on the market which will also do the job quite adequately. Always try to buy rugs which are of good quality. They will certainly last longer and stand up to washing. Night rugs are sure to get dirty and become stained with dung, and a cheap rug that tears and rots easily – and cannot stand up to being washed properly – will not last, and will turn out to be more expensive in the long run.

Some rugs have their own surcingles in addition to a breast strap, but others will require a well-padded roller to keep them in place. Some of the better night rugs have eyelets at the rear to allow for a tail string to prevent the rug from sliding forward. Rollers should always be fitted very carefully. They are usually about four to five inches wide, and can be made of hemp webbing, jute webbing, wool webbing or leather.

If a horse is stabled he will also need a good blanket to go under the night rug in winter. This can be expensive and these rugs are usually priced according to their weight.

An anti-sweat rug is not only useful in the stable when a horse has returned from exercise and is still sweating up, but is a very handy rug to have to hand when travelling. It is made of large cotton mesh, and works on the same principle as a string vest by creating air pockets next to the horse's body, forming insulation which stops him from becoming chilled. These rugs should always be used with an additional top sheet, otherwise the insulating air pockets cannot be formed, and the rug is of little use – except perhaps to keep off the flies! It should be kept in place with a roller because it will tear easily if the horse rolls – and the rug becomes displaced.

The wool day rug is like the night rug in shape, but it is available in different colours and bindings. You can have your initials sewn on either side of the rug – at the bottom end corner. These rugs look smart, particularly for travelling.

Summer sheets help to keep away dust and flies. They are made of cotton or linen and, like all the other rugs, need to be kept in place with a surcingle or roller. Horses travelling can also do with the extra protection of a tail guard – made of soft leather or canvas. It goes over the tail bandage and is fastened on to the roller.

New Zealand rugs have become almost a necessity because they not only provide protection for a horse or pony which has been trace-clipped and is at grass, but they also give sufficient warmth and covering for a hunter to be turned out into a field when the weather is reasonably good and it is not possible for him to be exercised. New Zealand rugs must be fitted carefully because – being made of strong waterproof canvas and lined with blanketing – they can slip and cause chafing around the neck area when a horse rolls. Care should be taken when removing the rugs to undo the leg straps first, and buckle them out of harm's way. New Zealand rugs require regular attention because they lead a hard life, having to withstand wind and weather, and being brushed against branches and hedgerows. The leather straps need regular greasing or they will become too hard, and the fastening hooks will also require oiling to avoid corrosion.

In Britain rugs and stable rugs are measured from the centre of the breast to the back of the rug, and usually range in size from about 1.2m (4ft) to 1.8m (6ft).

an anti-sweat sheet

a Lavenham rug

a New Zealand rug

a day rug

a summer sheet

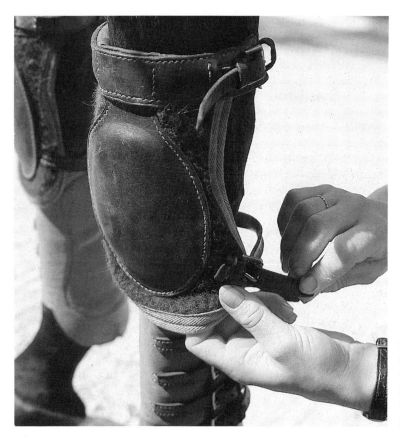

Left: knee caps or knee guards must be fitted when transporting a horse or pony. Ensure that when fastened there is sufficient room to give freedom of movement.

Bandages and boots

The types of bandages and boots required depend not only on the type of work you want a horse to do – and whether this will involve travelling – but also on his behaviour when jumping or in fast work. The main function of boots and bandages is to protect the legs against injury and to provide some support to the tendons. Brushing, when the inside of the leg, usually in the region of the fetlock joint, knocks against the opposite foot; and over-reaching, when the hind toes strike into the back part of the foreleg, can often be caused by poor shoeing producing a faulty action. This is not always the case, however, and the use of boots or bandages to prevent these types of injuries from occurring will then become a necessity.

Jumpers also sometimes need protection against the knocks they receive when hitting an obstacle, particularly when schooling, and this can take the form of either bandages, boots and jumping kneecaps, or sometimes all three. There are also special boots to protect all four legs of polo ponies from being struck by either a stick or the ball.

The lighter type of five-strap leather or felt brushing boot will provide adequate protection against occasional brushing,

Right: over-reach boots help protect the heels when galloping and jumping.

although one of the simplest and yet most effective anti-brushing devices is the rubber ring. When a horse is in fast work the point of his fetlock at the rear can come into contact with the ground and, if that happens, a heel boot will be needed. Over-reaches when jumping mostly occur low down on the heel. The best protection against this is the rubber over-reach boot which should be made of almost pure rubber so that it is elastic enough to pull over the hoof but small enough to fit snugly on the foot without revolving. A more dangerous form of injury can occur about the joint and in the back of the tendon. To prevent this a tendon boot should be worn. This has a strong pad at the rear, shaped to the leg, which will also help to support the tendon. Shin boots are also used on jumpers to protect their front and hind legs.

When travelling, felt hock boots safeguard a horse against banging his hocks on the side of the box, and travelling kneecaps, which are sometimes also used at exercise, will give protection to a horse's knees. They should, however, be loose enough to give freedom of movement.

Bandages come into two categories. Those of the stretch variety, which give support under working conditions, and those that provide warmth and protection when travelling. Exercise

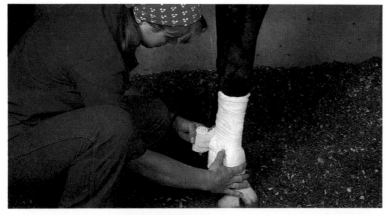

Left: exercise bandages, made of a material which has some stretch, gives support under working conditions. These are fitted over a gauze, gamgee or other protective tissue.

Right: the correct sequence for fitting exercise bandages.

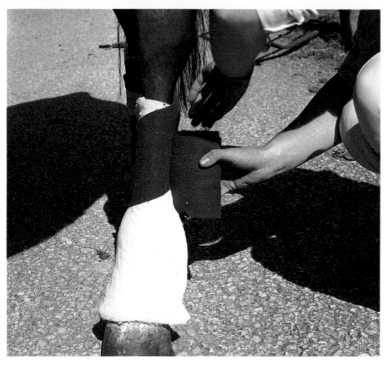

Above: fitting a tailguard gives added protection when transporting a horse or pony. *Right:* the tailguard correctly fitted.

and working bandages, which give a degree of stretch, must always by put on over gamgee tissue, and should be sewn in place when being used for cross-country riding or eventing.

Some riders now prefer a type of elasticated sock – rather like the surgical stocking sometimes worn by men and women. They are made in various shapes and sizes, and can be used for veterinary purposes to hold leg dressings in place.

Working bandages, used on the front legs, are put on between the knee and the fetlock joint, and on the hind legs between the fetlock and the hock, whereas stable and travelling bandages, which are made of wool, envelope the whole joint, and are sometimes put on over protective foam rubber pads.

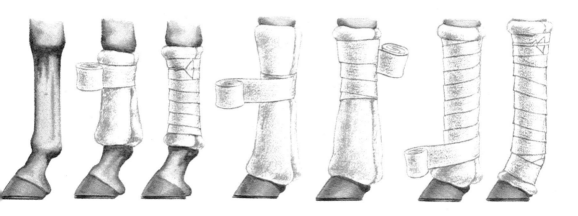

Artificial aids

Finally let us take a look at three of the artificial aids we have not yet mentioned, namely whips, canes and spurs. There are a wide variety of whips produced for various uses and at various prices, ranging from the cheaper type of general purpose whip with a fibreglass centre, to the hunting whips with their plaited leather thongs and cord lashes.

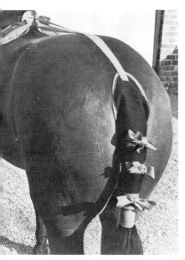

Sticks or canes covered with leather are popular for showing, and are perhaps better than a whip for the novice rider because they can also help maintain the correct hand position. The maximum length of stick allowed when show jumping is 76cm (30in).

Spurs are always worn with hunting boots, but if spurs are worn for jumping they must be as laid down in the Rules of the British Show Jumping Association. These read:

1. Spurs of excessively severe design are not to be worn. Such designs include spurs with necks in excess of 3cms (1.2ins) long, spurs with necks set on the inside of the heel, spurs with rowel diameters in excess of 1cm (0.4ins) and spurs with roughened or cutting edges.

2. Spurs are only to be worn in the traditionally correct manner, with the curve of the neck of the spur directed downwards.

3. The misuse of spurs is an offence, but riders must also take care that the manner in which they use their spurs does not offend the public.

4. In pony competitions, only blunt spurs not exceeding 3cms (0.8ins) long are permitted. Pointed, sharp and rowelled spurs are forbidden in these competitions.

5. Spurs made of plastic are not allowed.

8
Saddling and unsaddling

AFTER YOU HAVE CAUGHT and groomed your horse or pony he will be ready for his saddle and bridle. Make sure, however, that your smartly groomed pony is securely tied up before you leave him to go and fetch his tack. If you do not you may return to find that he has either wandered off, or has got down and had a good roll!

Check that saddle and bridle are ready for use before leaving the tack room. It is far easier to check a saddle on a saddle rack than when it is on the back of a fidgety pony.

Make sure that the stirrup irons and leathers are secure on the saddle – with the irons run up – and that the girth is already attached to the girth tabs on the off-side of the saddle. It should be laid across the top of the saddle.

The bridle should already have been adjusted so that it will be large enough to fit over the pony's head. If it is too small, alter the straps or find a larger bridle.

Good saddles and bridles are expensive and they need to be carried properly to prevent them from being damaged by being dragged along the floor or scraped against a wall. The easiest way is to hold the saddle with the front arch in the crook of your elbow so that you can carry the bridle over the same shoulder leaving your other hand free to open doors or deal with the pony. Some people prefer to carry the saddle along their thigh – with their hand in the front arch to hold it in place. It is mainly a matter of deciding which way is the most comfortable.

Approach the pony from the near side, and speak to him so that he knows you are there.

If the pony wears a martingale, put this on first, but if he only has a saddle and bridle it is correct to put the saddle on before the bridle. There is a very good reason for this. The saddle – providing it fits correctly – will settle into a pony's back, and the heat from his body will help to warm the underneath part before you mount.

Many horses and ponies blow themselves out when the saddle is being put on. This is because they think the saddle will be done up too tightly, and they take a deep breath to guard against it.

Never tighten the girth immediately. How would you like a

Right: it is best to carry a saddle with the front arch in the crook of the left elbow. Some riders carry the bridle in the left hand; others carry the bridle over the left shoulder, leaving their right arm free.

Above: when putting on a saddle see that it is correctly positioned, after having made certain that the hairs under the saddle are lying smoothly.

Left: doing up the girth.

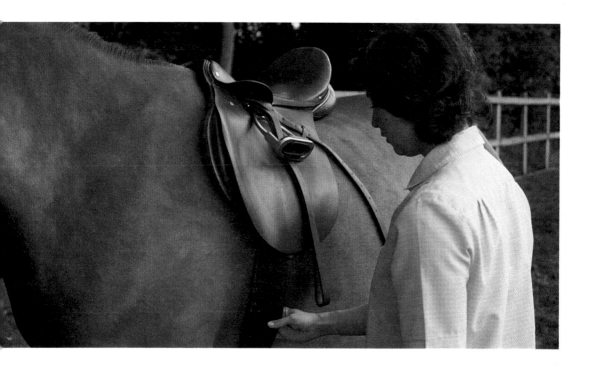

Above: never attempt to tighten the girth to its fullest extent when preparing prior to mounting. But do make sure it is tight enough to prevent it slipping as you climb up into the saddle. Final adjustment to the girth will be made after you are seated.

cold saddle put on your back and tightened up all in one go? You would hate it . . . and so will a pony. When you place the saddle on his back, take it in the crook of your left arm, and put it well forward of his withers, then slide it back into position, making sure that the hair underneath the saddle is lying smoothly.

Always keep near a pony's shoulder so that you will be out of harm's way if he does kick out for any reason. You will also be less likely to be in a position to get a nip.

Check that the sweat flap is down and, before doing up the girth, let it drop loose and walk round the front of the pony to the off side to make sure that nothing is ruffled up under the saddle flap. Then go back to the near side and keeping your own shoulder close to the pony's shoulder, tighten the girth just enough to hold the saddle firm, making sure that you have not pinched any of his skin. When you are ready to mount up and you tighten the girths, there should be approximately the same number of holes on either side.

Next take hold of the bridle which should have been hung up out of harm's way. If you have to saddle up in a field, without anywhere to hand the bridle, you can always keep it out of the way by putting it over your left shoulder. Hold the bridle with your left arm under the browband and headpiece, so that the browband is nearest to your elbow. Then put the buckles of the reins in front of the headpiece on your left forearm, leaving both hands free to undo your pony's head rope.

As soon as you do this he will usually try and put down his

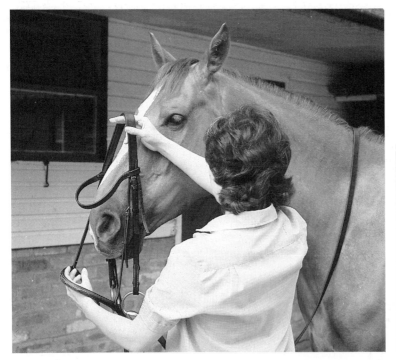

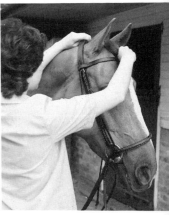

Above, left: bringing the bridle up over the horse's head must be started before (*left*) attempting to introduce the bit *Above:* once the bit is in position the bridle is adjusted, with the forelock brought over a straightened browband.

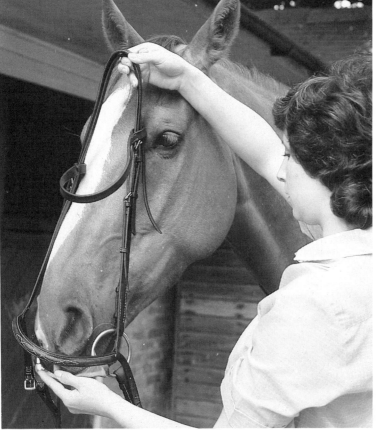

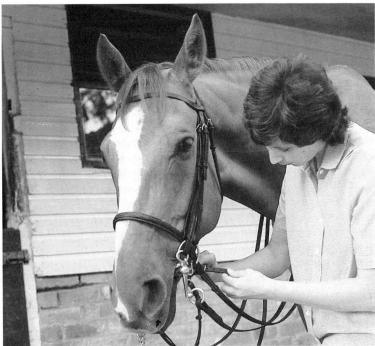

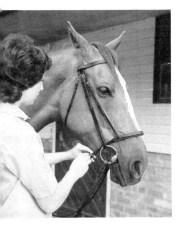

Above: before checking the position of the noseband the throatlash is fastened.

Above, right: the procedure for putting on a double bridle is as shown for the snaffle (see opposite page). The fastening of the chin-strap is done before fitting the curb chain.

head and look around for something to eat, but you must be ready for him. You cannot put a bridle on a pony when his head is on the floor.

After undoing his rope, put the reins over the pony's neck with your right hand so that you will have something to hold him with if he tries to walk away when you undo his headcollar or halter. If possible, place the halter on a convenient peg or hook, and try not to put it on the ground where it can be trodden on by you or the pony. There is no point in getting it damaged or dirty.

If you are in a stable or stall, turn the pony round into the light. Hold the headpiece of the bridle with your right hand, leaving yourself free to slide your left hand under the pony's mouth with the bit resting across your fingers and thumb.

The horse or pony may not want to open his mouth, but he will soon do so if you place your first finger between his lips on the off side until you can slide it into the gap where he has no teeth. You should be able to find this gap quite easily.

While you have been doing this your right hand should have been holding the headpiece close to his forehead, so that you will now be able to draw the bridle up over his head, and use your left hand to guide the bit into his mouth.

Once the bit is safely in a animal's mouth you will have both hands free to put the headpiece over each ear in turn. Never pull or jolt the bit into his mouth. Doing so will only make a pony more difficult on the next occasion.

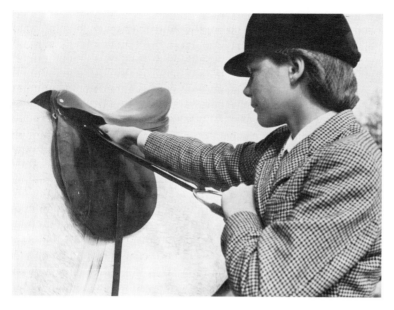

Left: checking the length of stirrup leathers before mounting.

Smooth down the mane and pull the forelock over the browband. Then run your fingers round under the headpiece to make sure that nothing is twisted and that the hair is lying correctly.

You will now be ready to do up the loose straps and run the ends through their keepers and runners. Start from the top of the bridle and work downwards, making sure that the noseband is inside the cheekpieces on both sides.

Finally, walk round to the horse's head to make certain that the browband is level, below the ears, but not touching them, and that the bridle is on straight with the holes in the cheekpieces level.

You should be able to get two fingers between the front of the face and the noseband, and the full width of your hand between the throatlash and his jawbone.

If you are not going to use the horse or pony immediately, leave the stirrups up on the saddle, and slide the ends of the reins underneath them in order to prevent him from rolling or putting his head down and pulling the reins over his head, where they can become trodden on and broken.

Some people, when they are putting on a bridle, prefer to put their right hand under a pony's jaw and up round his face just above his nostrils. Then, holding both cheekpieces in their right hand, they again use their left hand to open the pony's mouth and guide in the bit.

Both methods are correct. The second method probably gives a little more control in steadying the pony's head and preventing any sideways movement.

Taking off the saddle and bridle is quite simple. Starting with the saddle, run the irons up the stirrup leathers and tuck the ends of the loops through the irons to hold them in place. Take the reins over the pony's head and slip your left arm through the loop. Raise the saddle flap and undo the buckle of the girth, letting the end hang loose. If the pony is wearing a martingale, slip the loop from the girth and then, with one hand on the front arch of the saddle and the other on the cantle, or rear part of the seat, slide the saddle off the pony's back, on to your forearm so that the front arch rests in the crook of your elbow.

Next slide the girth, dirty side upwards, over the seat of the saddle, and place it down somewhere safe where it will not get knocked over or damaged.

Run your hands over the pony's back to make sure that there are not any lumps, and look under his belly to make sure that the girth has not rubbed any sore patches – known as girth galls. Then briskly pat the area where the saddle has been to help dry any sweaty patches and restore the circulation.

Now move round to the bridle, first making sure that you have a headcollar or halter ready to secure the pony with when the bridle has been removed.

Put your arm through the headcollar and let it rest on your shoulder out of the way, while you put the reins back over the pony's neck. This will give you something to hold on to and also with which to control the pony if he tries to move away.

In undoing the bridle remember that the opposite to putting on a bridle applies. You start at the mouth upwards, so that you begin with the curb chain, if the pony is wearing one, then undo the noseband followed by the throatlash.

When the straps of the noseband and the throatlash have been undone, place your left hand on the pony's face just above his nostrils, and use your right hand to slip the headpiece over his ears so that it can slide down on to your left forearm. Always ease the bit out of the pony's mouth. Never let it drop out suddenly or he may throw his head back and hurt his mouth. For the same reason a curb chain must be undone first.

Then slip the whole bridle, with the exception of the reins, on to your left shoulder, so that it is out of the way and you have both hands free to put the headcollar over the pony's head, and do up the strap before slipping the reins over his head.

Tie up the pony securely and check that the bit has not rubbed his mouth. If he seems cold, rub his ears gently between your thumb and fingers until they feel warm and dry.

Next, keeping the bridle, and martingale if there is one, over your left shoulder, pick up the saddle and girth and, holding the saddle with the front arch in the crook of your arm or along your thigh, take them to the tack room ready to be cleaned.

9
Mounting and dismounting

NOW THAT THE TIME HAS ARRIVED for you to get into the saddle and start to ride, clothing becomes important.

The four main articles of necessary clothing are a hard riding hat, a pair of jodhpurs or strong jeans to protect your legs from becoming sore, a jacket or a good, long-sleeved sweater to protect your arms, and strong boots or shoes (with a low heel) to prevent your feet from slipping through the stirrup irons.

Never mount a horse or pony unless you are wearing a hard hat and shoes with a heel, even if you are only planning to walk round the stable yard. Many riders have been injured unnecessarily because they ignored this basic commonsense rule.

Ponies cannot always be relied upon to stand quietly while their rider climbs into the saddle, and it is consequently important for you to learn to mount in such a way that you will be able to swing yourself up into the saddle without getting left behind if a pony suddenly moves.

Because cowboys ride in saddles with high pommels they have to mount facing a horse's head. With a European type of saddle the reverse is the case. Always stand ready to mount with your shoulder alongside the pony's shoulder, facing his tail. To begin with it is easier to learn to mount from the near side, but as you become more experienced you should be able to get on to your pony from either side.

Before getting into the saddle it is as well to check that your stirrup leathers are the correct length, so that once you are mounted you will be able to put your feet home in the stirrups and be ready for any move a pony may make. Do this by standing facing the saddle and pulling the stirrup irons down to the bottom of the leathers. Then clench your fist and place the knuckles of your right hand on the stirrup bar of the saddle. With your left hand hold the stirrup leather and iron up to your right armpit. If the leathers are the correct length the stirrup iron should just reach into your armpit. Although some people like to ride longer or shorter than others, this is still a very good way of judging the correct length while you are on the ground.

Having made sure that your stirrup irons are down and the

leathers are correct lift the saddle flap and check that the girth is tight enough to prevent the saddle from slipping when you put your weight in the stirrup. While you are doing this it is as well to see that the girth is not pinching any part of a pony's skin and that the buckle guards are in place to protect the saddle flap from the buckles. You will probably have to put the girths up another hole once you are in the saddle, so leave some spare holes free under the buckle guard.

When you are ready to mount, stand with your left shoulder alongside the pony's near shoulder, and take the reins and stick in your left hand. The reins should be short enough for you to control the pony if he moves forward, separated ready for riding with the off-side rein slightly shorter than the nearside. In this way, if he moves, the reins will steer him to the right, and his body will be brought round towards you, making it easier for you to get your right leg across the saddle.

Place your left hand holding the reins in front of the withers. When they are learning some people also like to take a grip of the mane. Then, holding the iron steady with the right hand, put your left foot into the stirrup. Press down the toes under the girth and pivot your body round until your are facing the pony. With your right hand seize the waist of the saddle on the far side and spring lightly upwards. As you do so, swing your right leg over the pony's back, taking care that your foot does not give him a bang on his quarters and cause him to jump forward. As your leg comes over, move your right hand to the front of the pommel and allow your body to sink gently into the saddle. You will then be able to place your right foot quietly into the stirrup iron, and have your pony under control.

Once you are safely in the saddle it is important to check your girth once again, and it may also be necessary to make some alteration to the length of your stirrup irons. Whether you are altering your girths or your stirrup leathers, you should never

Right: once in the saddle the girths should again be checked and, if necessary, tightened.

Far right: the feet should be kept in the stirrup irons while the leathers are adjusted.

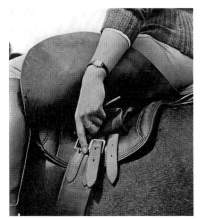
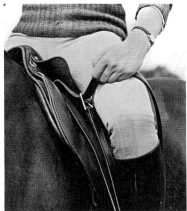

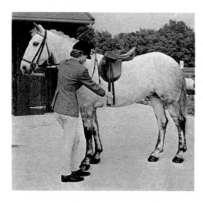
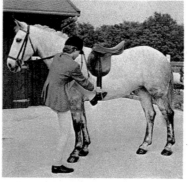

take your foot out of the stirrups. To deal with the girth, put the reins in one hand and bring your left leg forward until you can lift the saddle flap. Check the girth with your fingers, and if it needs tightening take each girth strap in turn and, having first loosened the buckle, pull it up a hole using your first finger to guide it into place. When both buckles are securely in position pull down the buckle guard and let the saddle flap fall back into place. You will then be able to take up your correct position in the saddle.

Altering the length of the stirrups is also quite easy. To change the left stirrup, put the reins in the right hand, and take hold of the spare end of the stirrup leather with the left. By placing your

Left: neatly illustrated is the way to mount and dismount.

thumb on top of the buckle, steer the tongue of the buckle with your first finger using the other three fingers to hold the spare end of the leather. As soon as the tongue becomes disengaged guide it into the correct hole. Then move the buckle until it fits snugly against the bar of the saddle by pulling down on the inside leather, and pressing down the stirrup iron. You should get into the habit of being able to alter the length of your stirrups from the saddle without looking down.

When you want to dismount, remember that you must first of all remove both your feet from the stirrups. Only when using a Western saddle would one dismount with a foot in the stirrup.

After ensuring that both feet are clear of the stirrup irons, lean forward and place your left hand, which should also be holding the stick, on the pony's neck. Then, placing your right hand on the pommel of the saddle, bend your right knee and vault off, making sure that you do not kick the pony as you bring your right leg over his back. Land gently on your toes, clear of your pony's front legs, and you will then be able to use your right hand to take a firm hold of the reins close up to the bit.

You will no doubt have seen some riders dismounting by throwing their leg over their pony's withers and sliding to the ground. This may look clever, but it is really very foolish because in doing so they have to let go of the reins and lose control of their pony, with the result that if he does move suddenly they can take a nasty fall.

Right: a stick or cane should point in the direction of the horse's opposite ear.

10
The seat

YOUR SEAT ON A HORSE OR PONY is important, not only because of the way you look, but also because of the control a good seat will give you over an animal's movements.

Good horsemen ride most of the time by balance and poise, and they keep their position by a combination of balance, suppleness and grip. They sit in the centre and lowest part of the saddle and, although remaining supple, are always in a position to grip quickly when they feel themselves becoming unbalanced.

The first essential for any rider is to acquire a good, strong seat which is completely independent of the reins. Regular practice. will help, but the correct length of stirrup leather is important. Beginners frequently ride with their stirrups too short. If you practice riding for a while without stirrups, stretching your legs and toes as far as they will go, you will find that you will be able to get lower in the saddle, and probably need to lengthen your leathers when you start riding with stirrups once again.

As you start to get the feel of a pony you should begin to develop a firm seat well down in the saddle. The upper part of your body should be upright, but it must always remain supple, particularly at the waist, because stiffness in one part of the body will quickly produce muscular contractions in another. Your head should be erect with your shoulders square so that you can look straight between the pony's ears.

Keep your knees and thighs close to the saddle. Learning the correct position will enable you to develop a natural grip downwards and inwards. Your knees and ankles must remain supple because stiffness in these joints will also cause stiffness in the upper part of your body.

The lower part of your legs should be kept slightly behind the girth so that they can be used to apply the 'aids' without any sudden movement. If your legs are in the correct position the stirrup leathers will be perpendicular to the ground. It is particularly important to develop a correct position for the lower part of your legs because an incorrect one will only create bad balance.

Your heels should be below the level of your toes to enable the

Right: riding without stirrups helps the rider to get lower in the saddle.

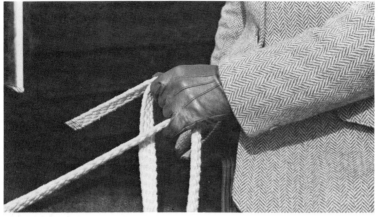

Left: holding the reins in one hand.

important muscles on the inside of your thighs to remain taut, and your knees to be low on the saddle. Keep your knees and toes pointing towards the front. Turning out your toes will tend to make you grip with the back of your calves.

The stirrups should be held on the balls of your feet so that your ankles can remain supple. You can always thrust your feet home in the stirrups when necessary.

Let your arms hang naturally down to the elbows, lightly touching your hips. Your forearms should form a straight line along the reins to the pony's mouth. Keep your hands just above and in front of the saddle, with the thumbs upwards and your wrists and fingers supple enough to be able to follow the movements of the pony's head and neck.

The reins should normally be held in both hands but there will be occasions when you need to hold them in only one hand. If you are using a snaffle or single-rein bridle and you want to hold both reins in your left hand, take the right rein between either the first and second fingers or the first finger and thumb. The left rein should then be held outside the fourth finger with the slack part of the reins across the palm of your left hand.

To hold the reins in both hands, place your right hand on the right rein with the rein outside your little finger and take it from the left hand. Let the slack part of the reins pass between the finger and thumb of each hand.

Some riders, however, prefer to hold the reins between the little finger and third finger because it gives them a better grip.

If your horse or pony is wearing a double bridle with two reins, these can be held in the left hand by placing your little finger between the two left reins and your second finger between the two right reins. The slack of the reins can then pass between your first finger and thumb.

To take the reins in both hands, divide them with the little finger of each hand with the bridoon or snaffle rein on the outside.

Right: the illustration shows the rider sitting correctly by being well down in the saddle.

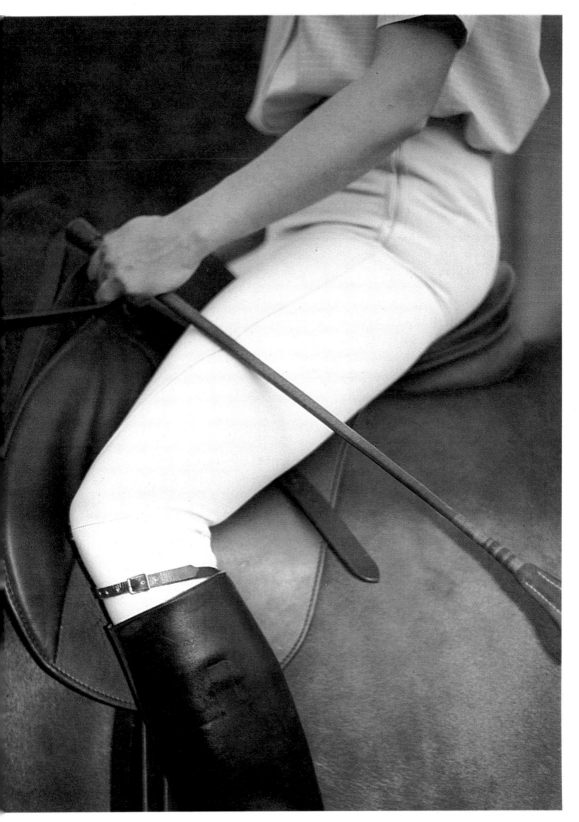

11
The 'aids'
– the rider's signalling system

A RIDER CONVEYS HIS INTENTIONS to his horse or pony by way of 'aids' and these are the universal signals which you and your pony must learn to understand. They must be given clearly and accurately, so that he will change pace or direction smoothly.

The term 'aids' not only refers to the signals you give to indicate your wishes, but also to the means at your disposal for making signals.

There are *natural* aids, given by the hands, legs, body and voice, and *artificial* aids, where the rider uses a stick, spurs and items of saddlery, like a martingale.

When learning you should concentrate on the natural aids, starting with **the body** and making full use of the back muscles and seat. By bracing the back musles you can then straighten your spine, pushing forwards and downwards through the seat, knees and heels.

The legs can then be used to increase pace and energy by pressing the thighs and the inside of the calves against the horse's sides. When this is done the toes should only be turned slightly outwards, making sure that the heels are not dug into the horse's ribs.

As a means of controlling the hindquarters, remember your legs can either be used separately or together in partnership with the hands.

Through the reins, **the hands** can either regulate the energy created by the legs, control the horse's forehand, or guide and alter his rhythm and pace.

The voice is an aid which many novice riders only remember in an emergency. It should, however, be used to encourage, soothe or to check a movement. It is also effective as a means of urging a horse into obeying an important command. One aid, however, is of little use without the other. They should be used together.

Artificial aids must be used carefully and only when a rider is fully aware of their correct use.

A stick or cane looks correct and is easiest to handle when about one quarter protrudes in front of the hand, and points in the direction of the horse's opposite ear. You should practise changing the stick quickly and smoothly from one hand to the other. Being able to do this efficiently is important when schooling a horse over jumps or when a horse shies at an obstacle which has to be passed. It should be used just behind your leg, and only when the horse fails to respond to your legs.

The hunting whip – which must always have a thong and lash – is carried in the same way as a stick – with the hook to the rear, pointing towards the ground. It is useful for opening gates, or for keeping hounds away from a horse's legs by holding it outwards so that the thong and lash hang downwards.

Spurs must *never* be used as a method of punishment. They are purely an aid to make a horse lighter and more responsive to the legs. In the early stages of learning to ride spurs should not be worn. Later, with more experience and understanding, they should be applied gently, with the inside of the spur against the horse's side. Remember your toes must not be turned outward, or the backs of the spurs will be brought into contact with the horse with very unpleasant results.

Learning to apply the aids correctly takes time. It requires a knowledge of technique as well as some natural ability. To get the best results the signals given to a horse must be light but positive. With a well-trained animal they should be given in such a way that they are very difficult for an onlooker to discern.

Below: the horse's hindquarters are controlled by the legs in partnership with the hands.

12
The paces or gaits

ONCE YOU KNOW HOW TO SIGNAL your intentions to your horse or pony in a way in which he will understand, you should be able to move smoothly through the paces from a walk to a trot, and then on to a canter and gallop, and finally back to a halt.

When you want a pony to walk forwards, squeeze slightly behind the girth with your legs and urge him on with your seat and back while at the same time keeping a light contact with his mouth. To achieve the best results you will need to gain complete harmony between your body, legs and hands.

As a pony walks forward, do not alter the position of your body, but look ahead in the direction in which you are going and move in rhythm with the natural movement of the pony.

To move from the walk to the trot, sit down in the saddle and use the same instructions or aids as you would to change from the halt to the walk.

There are two ways of riding at the trot. There is the sitting trot, when your seat remains in the saddle, and the rising trot, when you rise in time with the motion of the pony. A horse or pony trots in two-time with the off fore and near hind legs moving together, and the near fore and the off hind legs moving together. You are said to be riding on the right diagonal when your seat returns to the saddle as a pony's off fore and near hind legs touch the ground together. You can change the diagonal by sitting down in the saddle for an extra beat before starting to rise again.

The rising trot should be an easy motion for you and the pony, without any jerks or bumps. Incline the upper part of your body forward slightly and keep the small of your back supple. Do not make an effort to rise in the saddle, but let the pony do all the work, leaving you to take the weight on your knee and ankle joints.

If your back is stiff and hollow your stomach will be pushed forward as you rise, and there will be a tendency for you to pull yourself up with the reins. Practice will enable you to trot easily and without any noticeable exertion.

Sitting to the trot means maintaining contact with the saddle on both diagonals – not an easy task for a beginner! But it will

Walk

With four distinct beats to each stride the walk is said to be in 'four-time'. At this pace, which should be active and energetic, the sequence is near hind; near fore; off hind; off fore.

strengthen your gripping muscles, and thus help you to develop a good, secure and independent seat. By sitting down and keeping a light contact with the pony's mouth you will be able to use your legs to squeeze him forward into a canter.

A pony is said to be cantering 'true' or 'united' when his leading foreleg and leading hindleg are both on the same side. He is cantering 'disunited' when his leading hind leg is on the opposite side to his leading foreleg.

Remember that the pace of the canter is three-time so that there are three distinct beats to each stride. The upper part of your body should give in time to the rhythm and motion of the pony, and your seat should remain close to the saddle. It may sound difficult, but you will soon learn to go with your pony.

If your back is stiff and rigid you will bump up and down in the

Trot

The two types of trot are the rising trot and sitting trot. This pace, which should remain even throughout, gives two beats to each stride, and the sequence is near hind and off fore together; off hind and near fore together.

saddle. Getting your weight too far forward off the bones of your bottom is another common fault which must be mastered.

When you have learnt to sit easily at the canter you should learn to make the pony strike off with the correct leg.

If you are going to canter to the left the pony should lead with his near foreleg, and if you are cantering to the right he should lead with his off fore.

To make him lead with his off fore, put the pony into a trot and flex him slightly to the right with your right rein, sitting well down in the saddle as you do so. Then squeeze with both legs, keeping your left leg a little further back than your right. The object of keeping your left leg behind the girth is to prevent the pony's quarters from swinging out and also to let him know exactly what is required of him.

To canter with the near fore leading, reverse the process so that you flex the pony to the left with your left rein, and sitting well down in the saddle, squeeze with your legs keeping your right leg behind the girth.

From the canter you can use your legs in conjunction with your hands to urge the pony on into a gallop. Either sit well down in the saddle and drive the pony forward with your seat and legs, or adopt a forward position so the weight of your body is taken on your knees and stirrups. Your seat should be off the saddle, with your body leaning forward over your hands, and your weight poised over the centre of gravity.

It is easy to maintain this position providing you keep a firm and even contact with the pony through the bit.

You should remember that your hands must be sensitive to every reaction in the pony's mouth. They should always be used in conjunction with your legs and back, and be held on either side

Canter
There are three beats to the canter. At this pace, with the off fore leading, the sequence is near hind; off hind and near fore together; off fore. When cantering a horse should appear balanced and rhythmic, and light on his feet.

of the pony's withers. When slowing the pony down, close both legs into his sides, straighten your spine and drive him up into what is termed a 'resisting' hand. Your pony should decrease pace smoothly and hold his head steady. When he halts he should be made to stand squarely on all four legs. As soon as he has obeyed your command, relax both legs and the pressure on the reins.

There will be occasions when you will want the pony to rein-back. Before asking him to do so make sure that he is standing straight, with his jaw relaxed, and his head held fairly low.

Push him up into his bit by pressure from your legs and seat, but instead of yielding with your hands, as you would if you wanted him to walk forward, retain the pressure on the reins. The pony should rein-back in two-time and move in a straight line. As soon as he has taken the necessary number of steps backwards ease the reins and allow him to come to a halt, before going forward once more.

13
Clipping, trimming and plaiting

EVERY HORSE OR PONY required to carry out fast work during the winter, when his coat is heavy, needs to be clipped, but the extent of the clip will depend on the type of work and also whether the animal is being stabled. If the hair is left long, the animal will sweat up and lose condition. There is an old saying that riding an unclipped horse is like expecting it to run a race in an overcoat.

A horse turned out with a New Zealand rug will usually require a **trace clip** or a blanket clip. In the case of the trace clip, which was very popular for harness horses some years ago, the hair is removed from the under surface of the body and along the windpipe area of the neck. In some cases a narrow line is also run up the quarters to the tail. The hair is left long on the legs and back, but there are three variations of the clip – high, medium and low – according to how high the hair is left on the sides. The **blanket clip** is similar, but the hair on the neck and head is removed and cut square where a blanket would lie across the withers and shoulders.

A stabled hunter should be fully clipped out with the exception of his legs, the triangle at the top of his tail, and the saddle patch. This is known as the **hunter clip** and the hair on the legs is left long as a protection against injuries from thorns, as well as cracked heels and mud fever. The saddle patch is left to absorb some of the sweat and to alleviate pressure and chafing.

Alternatively, horses can be given a **full clip** when they are clipped right out – with the exception of the triangle above the tail.

There is another type of clip sometimes seen on the race-course known as the **chaser clip** – when all the hair is removed from the head and the lower part of the neck and body up the sides to the area where the saddle flaps would be. The hair on the top part of the body – from behind the ears on the neck through to the tail – is left long to provide protection. Sometimes the clip is taken up the quarters and rounded-off, making it look very smart and workmanlike.

Undoubtedly clipping makes a great difference to a horse's

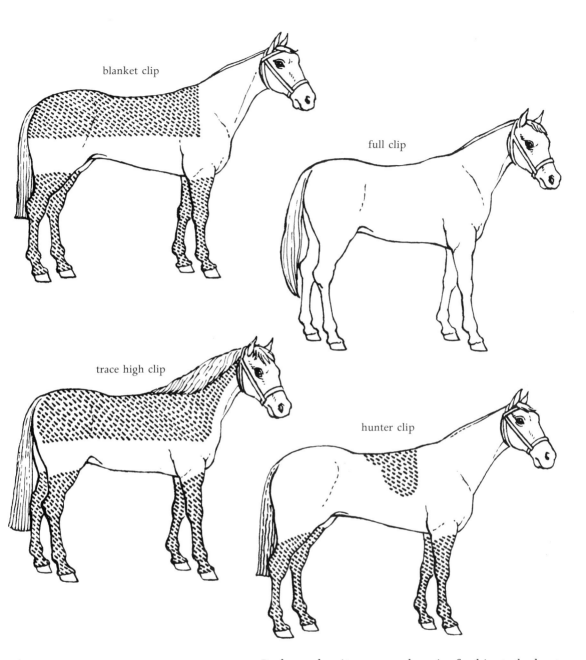

blanket clip

full clip

trace high clip

hunter clip

appearance. It also makes it very much easier for him to be kept clean and tidy. Horses and ponies should get their first clip of the season in late autumn. They usually start to grow their winter coats at the end of the summer when the coat begins to look dull and rough, and it should then be left until the winter coat becomes properly established (about a month to six weeks later), before any of it is removed.

In the case of horses and ponies which have been clipped right out, it is quite usual to leave the legs and saddle patch on with the second clip, which is done just before the onset of winter. This

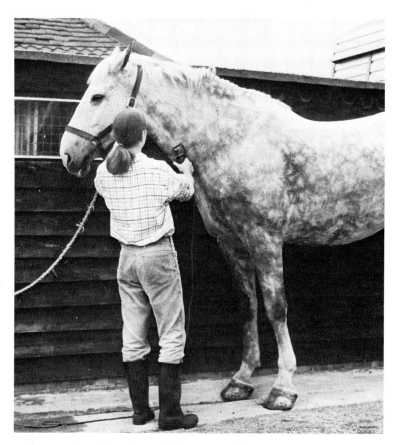

Left: rubber boots should be worn when clipping and the electric lead kept away from the horse's feet. In cold weather a blanket should be used to keep the horse warm.

makes them look less hairy than they would if their legs had been left unclipped in the autumn. The positioning of the saddle patch can alter the appearance of an animal. Care should consequently be taken to ensure that that patch is in the right place and also clipped round evenly. One way of doing this is to clip round a numnah. Always remember that a clipped-out horse will feel the cold at exercise early in the morning, with the result that he may well be inclined to buck and play about. A fresh horse and sleepy rider can soon be parted!

In mid-winter a horse can be given a light clip to remove any 'cat' hairs which otherwise look so long, coarse and unsightly, as well as collecting mud. If the animal has a coarse coat it is far better to clip fairly frequently, than to clip too close the first time and cause him to feel cold. Horses do not like shocks to their systems any more than humans do, and they should never be clipped if the weather is very wet or frosty or if there is a cold wind. A cold horse will never be a contented horse.

Clipping is an art which can be acquired quite easily providing you follow some simple rules. The first rule is never be in a hurry. If you make a mistake you cannot put back the hair . . . and many a trace clip has ended as a full clip because the groom was trying to go too quickly. Make sure that your equipment is working properly, and that you have a spare set of sharp blades in case a tooth becomes broken, or the pair already in the clippers becomes blunt. You should, in any case, have a coarser pair of blades which will be needed for the legs.

There are two types of electric clipper. There is the lighter hand type with the motor handle, which is easy to use and which will be perfectly adequate providing you do not allow it to become overheated, and your horse has a normal coat which is not too thick. The alternative is the heavy-duty type normally used in the larger professional stables where the clippers are in more frequent use. This has a powerful clipper which hangs from a wall bracket and has a flexible shaft to which the cutting head is attached.

Whichever type of machine you use, remember to maintain it properly, and follow a few commonsense rules to ensure that it is only asked to function under the circumstances for which it was designed. Properly serviced electric clipping machines rarely give trouble, but any that are neglected can become a constant nuisance.

Before starting, make sure that your horse or pony is as dry and as clean as his coat will permit. Tie him up with a halter attached to a loop of string fastened to the ring. If you are clipping him in his box, stack his bed along the walls, and sweep the centre of the floor clean and dry. It is important to remember that you are using an electric appliance, so that if your horse has steel shoes on a wet floor, and your clippers develop a fault, there is a risk of electrocution.

Always to wear rubber boots or rubber-soled shoes when clipping. If you feel the clippers vibrate or if they give off any shock, turn them of immediately at the mains switch, and don't use them again until the fault has been properly diagnosed and repaired.

You will not want your animal's hair to get in the way while you are working, and so before you clip plait up the mane with elastic bands, and double the tail up and enclose it in a tail bandage. Remember that it is easy to catch the mane or tail in the clippers and they need to be kept out of the way. Place a folded rug over the horse's back before starting – because a cold horse will be a fidgety horse and making clipping that much more difficult. Make sure he has a full hay net to keep him amused while you get on with the job.

When you plug into the socket and switch on at the mains, stand well back from your horse before switching on the clippers. Let them run free for a few moments so that he can get used to the noise and you can ensure that they are running smoothly. Then adjust the tension screw by turning it until the clipper speed slows down. Next, turn it up about half a turn to let it return to its normal speed, and run an oil can containing thin oil along the blades and in the oil holes. If the blades are too tight, the engine will be strained and become overheated. When you are satisfied that everything is in order, start on the hindquarters, keeping the blades running into the coat against the direction that it is growing and keep them at an angle, with the points slightly upwards so that they glide smoothly over the skin.

The height of the hair on the legs – unless you are clipping right out – is a matter of preference, but it is usual to clip the forelegs from the elbow to the natural groove by the chest, and the hind legs from the stifle (or just below) to a point about a hand's width above the hocks. You must get both sides even, working a little on one side and then moving over to the other. If you are trace clipping, lift the clippers to make a straight edge, and do not try to take the coat line too high all at once. Keep below the line you are aiming at to begin with – until you are sure that you have the correct height and that both sides will match. Move the rugs as you work to make sure your horse does not get cold. Remember to let the machine do the work so that all you have to do is guide the blades, and make sure that the coat line remains level.

Brush the coat regularly to remove the loose hairs. If you feel that the clippers are getting too hot, switch them off for a while. Use the time that they are cooling down to clear the hair out of the blades and re-oil them.

When it comes to doing the head and neck, slip the halter round his neck so that you are free to hold his head still with one hand while you use the clippers with the other. If a horse starts to play up, take your time doing his head, and if he refuses to settle down it is much better to use a twitch than to have a battle which you will almost certainly lose. A horse which is really hard to clip may need a veterinary surgeon to give him a tranquilliser. If you have to use a twitch, it should be placed on the nose below the nostrils, and held steady by a helper. Never ever use a twitch on the ear. To do so is cruel, and will make the horse much worse in the long run.

Never clip the hair from inside the ears or interfere with the long hair in the muzzle area. Care must be taken not to clip the mane or tail, and the clippers should not be used on the back of the tendons or fetlocks. If the hair will not pull easily, use scissors and a comb moving them upwards against the hair.

Heels can be trimmed with a comb and scissors or with a pair of hand clippers. These can also be used to take away the long coarse 'cat' hairs in the region of the jaw, between the chin groove and the throat.

After you have finished clipping, and checked that both sides

are the same, brush the coat thoroughly to remove any remaining loose hairs, unplait the mane, and take off the tail bandages before putting the rug straight. When you have made the horse comfortable, brush the stable floor, and give him an extra depth of bedding to help keep him warm. Then clean the clippers thoroughly before oiling them and putting them away ready for use next time.

After a horse has been clipped he will probably need trimming. The mane, tail, jaw, ears and heels will all need trimming from time to time. Manes should always be pulled or hogged. Pulling is done either to thin out a mane which is too thick and long or to make it lie flat. The longest hairs underneath should be removed, a few at a time, by winding them round a finger and giving a short, sharp pull. Never pull the top hairs, and on no account use the scissors or clippers for this purpose. You will need a brush to get rid of any tangles, and a comb to get the mane lying straight on its natural side. Work up the neck from the withers and then down again. Do a little at a time. If you remove too much you will only make the crest sore.

The length of the tail is usually a matter of preference, but a tail that is too long can hamper a horse, particularly when jumping, and it is usual to square off the tail so that the end reaches somewhere between the hocks and the fetlocks. A 'switch' tail is

Top: pulling the tail.

Above: trimming the tail.

Below: trimming the heels.

Right: pulling the mane.

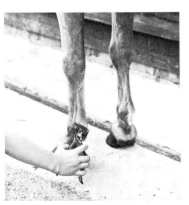

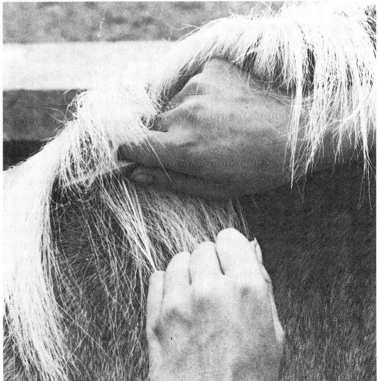

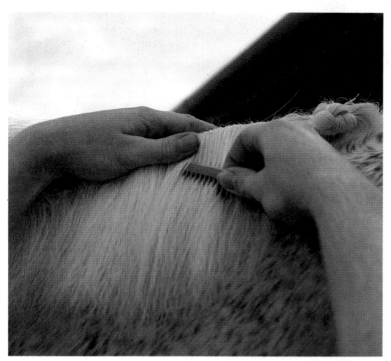

one which is allowed to come to a point, by brushing out the bottom until it becomes wispy. The top of the tail in the dock region can either be left long, so that it may be plaited, or it can be pulled a little at a time.

To pull a tail, first brush it straight with a body brush and remove all the tangles. Then, starting at the sides, take one or two hairs between your first finger and thumb, and slide the trimming comb up the other hairs so that those to be removed are uncovered. Then pass the centre finger over the hairs and, pressing down firmly with the comb, pull them out gently by the roots. Keep both sides even by taking out a few hairs at a time. The secret is to do it slowly, little by little. When the tail has been finished, a tail bandage should be put in place. If a horse is inclined to kick, tie him up so that his tail falls over the stable door, or better still, use a straw bale for protection. The process should not be painful to the horse. If it is you are either taking too many hairs at a time, or you are trying to do the job too quickly. The hairs of the mane and the tail will pull more easily when the pores of the skin are warm and open when he returns from exercise, or when the weather is warm.

Manes are plaited for neatness, to show off the neck and crest, and to train the hair to fall into place on the correct side, which is normally the off side. It is usual to have an odd number of plaits along the neck, and one for the forelock.

When a horse is hogged all the hairs of the mane and forelock

On these two pages are shown part of the procedure to be used when plaiting or braiding. *Left:* first comb the mane and select sufficient hair to make a plait. *Above:* the comb will keep any unplaited hair away from the job at hand. Begin the plait by working as close as possible to the roots of the hair.

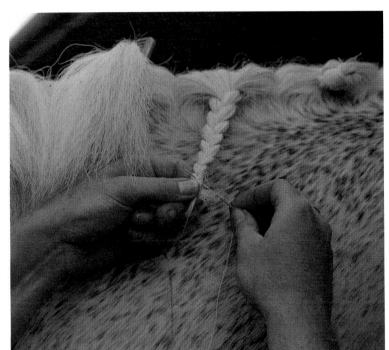

Above: each plait is made in the traditional way, and it is usual to have an odd number of plaits along the neck, with an additional one for the forelock. *Right:* having made the plait, and having seen that this is tightly finished, sew in the plait with a needle and thread.

are removed with the clippers. It can only be done properly when someone stands in front of the horse and gently forces his head down by taking hold of the ears so that the crest is stretched. Starting at the withers and working towards the poll, the whole of the mane is taken off, making sure that no unsightly line is left where the coat and crest meet. Hogging needs to be done about every three weeks, and once a mane has been hogged it will usually take at least two years to grow properly.

When the time comes to turn out a horse that has been clipped during the winter months, remember that he will have to be roughed off to prepare him for the change in environment and diet. This will usually take about two weeks. During that period his ration of concentrates needs to be reduced gradually, and fast work should stop so that his exercise is restricted to walking and trotting. The blankets should gradually be discarded, and he should be stabled at night without rugs for about a week before being turned out completely. The best time to do this is in early summer, preferably when the weather is mild and dry.

14
The horse's feet

THERE IS A WELL-KNOWN SAYING 'no foot, no horse' – and how true that is! Do not forget that the few square centimetres which go to make up the foot of a horse or pony have to support not only his own weight, and absorb the strain and concussion of galloping and jumping on various types of ground, but also the weight of a rider who may not always be in the correct place at the right time! Remember that when a horse is galloping or jumping he brings one forefoot down to the ground at a time, with the result that more than half a ton is supported on one small area. When this is borne in mind, it is quite remarkable that horses do not get more foot trouble.

Severe concussion or strain can cause inflammation. In other parts of the body this would show as a swelling, because extra blood is rushed to the affected area to help it to heal. In the case of a horse's foot, however, the damaged part is prevented from swelling by the box-like nature of the hoof. This can lead to all sorts of complications, until eventually the bones may become displaced, or deformed unless the trouble is treated properly. Even so some lameness in the foot cannot be dealt with effectively because it is not possible to reach the injured areas.

When you next pick up a horse's hoof, take a good look at the way in which it has been formed. Make sure you know the correct names of the various parts, so that you can describe them properly if you need to do so. The horse's foot is a highly sensitive organ inside its outer wall, and it can easily be damaged – a fact which many people unfortunately forget.

A number of different types of bone are encased inside the hoof, and they all have their own tendons, ligaments and blood vessels. Packed around these bones are layers of sensitive flesh known as laminae, a name you will probably recognise if you have ever had a pony with laminitis or fever of the feet. Although the wall and sole of the foot are rigid, the inner structure is able to move because of the rubber-like quality of the frog, that triangular wedge with a cleft in the centre, which is let into the back of the sole and acts as a shock absorber as well as helping the horse to grip. As his foot comes to the ground the frog takes a lot of the weight, in addition to absorbing the concussion. When that happens it depresses, forcing the ends of the walls outwards slightly, and making some movement of the inner structure possible. You can now see why it is so important to clean out a horse's feet regularly and to make sure that stones are not allowed to lodge between the frog and the wall. The frog is also important because it helps pump round the blood to improve the circulation.

Another important part of the hoof is the coronary band or coronet which divides the hoof from the skin and hair of the legs, and provides nourishment to the wall, so that it can grow properly. If, for any reason, the coronet becomes damaged, the wall will not grow as it should, and a bulge or split will develop in the crust. Any inflammation of the blood vessels in the foot, either because of poisoning or some other cause, will result in lameness, and the cause of the trouble must be dealt with quickly.

Inflammation is always present in all the injuries and diseases of the feet, and it is important for you to learn to recognise some of the more common ones. We have already referred to laminitis which is caused when the sensitive laminae, which surround the bones of the feet, become inflamed. This can be the result of concussion, either through too much trotting on the hard road or galloping on rock-hard ground. Most laminitis, however, is

Parts of the hoof.

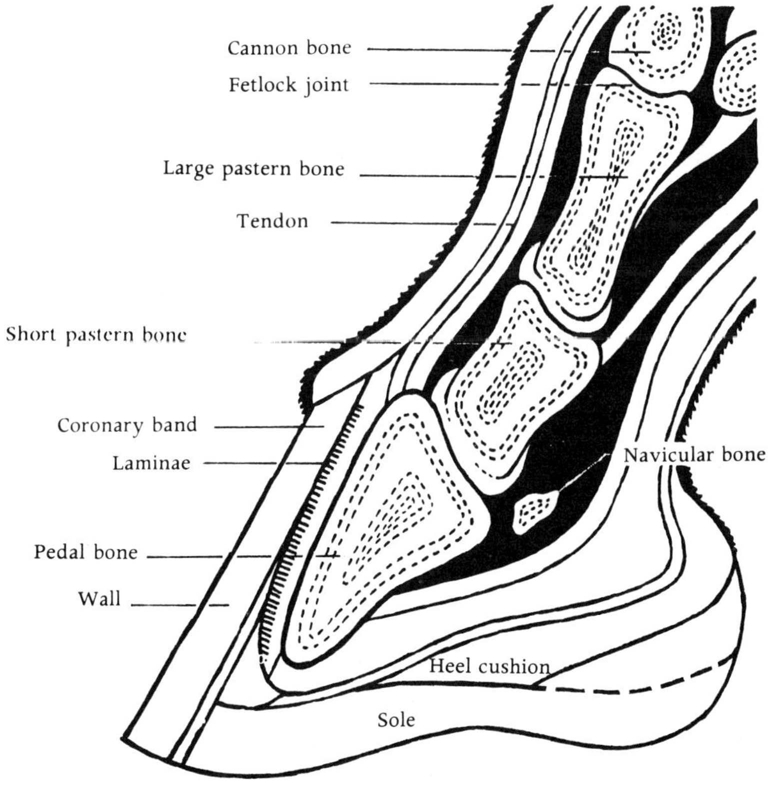

Cannon bone

Fetlock joint

Large pastern bone

Tendon

Short pastern bone

Coronary band

Laminae

Navicular bone

Pedal bone

Wall

Heel cushion

Sole

caused by incorrect feeding, and occurs in very fat and underworked horses and ponies, usually in the spring and early summer when the grass is particularly lush and rich. It can also occur in stabled horses who do not get enough exercise or horses which are given too much fast work before they are fit.

The disease rarely affects the hind feet, but attacks the front feet so that the animal will become both lame and unwilling to move. To relieve the intense pain in his feet, he will stand with them stuck out in front of his body, with his hind legs drawn forward underneath – rather as though he were leaning with his hindquarters against an imaginary wall. A veterinary surgeon should be sent for promptly, but while you are waiting for him to arrive, the animal's feet should be hosed with cold water and he should be given a bran mash containing about three ounces of salt.

If the trouble is not dealt with quickly irreparable damage may occur. Once a pony has had an attack of laminitis, care must be taken to see that he does not get another, since after the first he will be particularly susceptible to the disease. You can often see when a pony has had laminitis. The wall of the hoof will have become deformed, due to the bones being forced out of place by the swelling laminae inside the foot. Laminitis is one of the most common of all the foot troubles. It can be cured by rest and careful feeding, but far too many ponies are spoilt because of it.

Far more serious is navicular disease, which starts with inflammation of the navicular bone situated at the back of the foot, just above the frog. The inflammation can again be caused by too much jumping on hard ground, or by sudden strain. The disease is incurable, although some pain-deadening powders can bring temporary relief, because the inflammation will eat into the smooth surface of the navicular bone roughening it up, so that normal movement of the bone becomes impossible. At first the animal will appear intermittently lame.

Rest will improve the lameness, but the horse will go unsound again as soon as he is put into work. Eventually he becomes permanently lame. Being of an arthritic nature there is no effective cure, although he may be able to remain in work for some time, either by the use of powders, or by an operation known as 'de-nerving' when the veterinary surgeon cuts the plantar nerve at the back of the leg, making the foot insensitive to pain. This will not, however, prevent the disease from developing further, and the operation is never completely satisfactory for this reason.

Some forms of lameness in the foot are fortunately far less serious, and will quickly respond to the correct treatment. Bruising, for example, usually occurs through a horse putting the sole of his foot down hard on a sharp object such as a stone.

He will immediately appear lame, because the bruising will set up inflammation. This can usually be detected. By feeling his feet you will find that the injured foot will appear warmer than the others. The horse will also be unwilling to put any pressure on the foot, and show signs of pain if it is struck lightly with a hammer. The shoe will have to be removed and the injured area poulticed. If it does not respond quickly to treatment a veterinary surgeon should be called.

Other frequent causes of lameness are corns, caused by shoes pressing into the heels; sandcracks, splits in the wall of the foot; thrush, the disease of the frog caused by dirt and neglect; and seedy-toe, in which the sole of the foot separates from the wall, causing the horn to rot inside. Horses feet also sometimes pick up nails or other pieces of metal. These must be removed as quickly as possible, and the damaged area treated. If any lameness persists for more than a few days, don't hesitate any longer. Get professional advice.

However well your horse or pony is fed and looked after, it will be useless for any real work unless it is shod correctly. Horses have been shod since the times of early civilisation, and over the years a great deal of knowledge has been built up, not only on the action of the foot, but also on the best forms of shoeing.

Metal shoes have become accepted as the best form of shoe to protect a horse's feet, but in recent years other types of shoes have been tried, including various forms of plastic.

There are two systems of shoeing: hot shoeing – when the shoe is specially made and tried on hot, so that adjustments can be made before the shoe is finally cooled and nailed on, and cold shoeing – when a ready made shoe is fitted and altered as far as possible while cold. Hot shoeing is by far the most satisfactory. Whichever system is used there is always one golden rule which should be observed, however. The shoe should always be made to fit the foot, and not the foot made to fit the shoe.

Let us look at the six different stages of hot shoeing. To begin with there is the removal of the old shoe, when the blacksmith cuts off all the clenches with his metal buffer and driving hammer, and then levers the shoe off with pincers. Providing all the clenches have been cut off cleanly, there will be no damage to the wall of the foot when the shoe is removed.

The blacksmith then prepares the foot by cutting away the overgrowth of horn ready for the new shoe to be fitted. Before doing so, however, he must clean out the sole and frog, and make sure that they are both healthy. To cut back the wall he will use either a drawing knife, or toeing knife, or sometimes a horn cutter. Any ragged parts of the sole or frog will be trimmed as little as possible, and then he will use a rasp to level the foot to

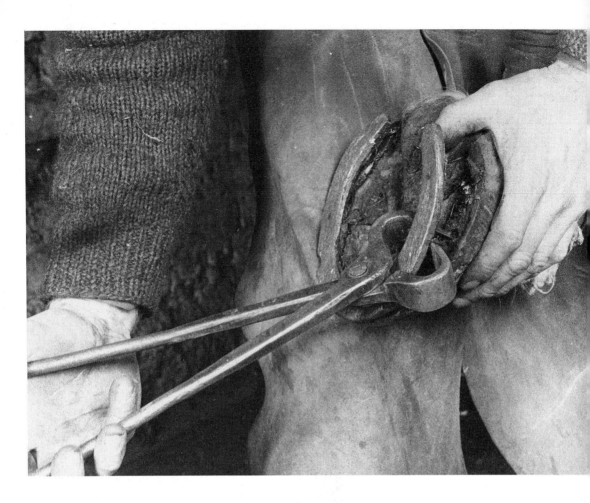

give a good bearing surface. If the surface is not level, strain will be put on the horse every time his foot touches the ground.

The process of making a new shoe is known as forging, and the weight and type of shoe selected will depend either on the nature of the work the horse is expected to do or whether there is any defect in the make-up or action of the horse which needs to be remedied. The solution could be a plain, stamped shoe which consists of an ordinary bar of iron, shaped and stamped with nail holes, and given a toe clip.

He may, however, choose a hunter shoe made of concave iron, to reduce the risk of it being sucked off in soft going and additionally to give more grip. If the horse is inclined to brush one leg against another he could use a featheredged shoe, where the inner part of the shoe has been 'feathered' to fit close in under the wall to reduce the risk of brushing. This type of shoe does not have nail holes along the inner branch.

For a horse or pony being rested at grass he would probably select half-length shoes or grass tips to stop the wall of the hoof from splitting at the toe.

Above: the blacksmith begins his work by removing the worn shoe, after having first 'cut-off' the clenches. At this time he will look at the condition of the foot and check the sole and the wall.

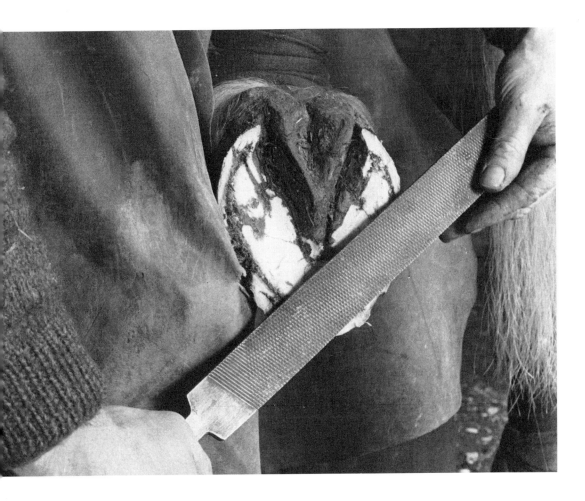

Above: before fixing a new shoe the sole of the foot must be rasped flat. Any unnecessary growth is removed by the blacksmith with a drawing or toeing knife.

If he decides on a normal shoe he will shape the iron, and then draw the clips and stamp and nail holes ready for the shoe to be fitted.

This has to be done while it is still hot, and so the blacksmith uses a pritchel – a pointed metal tool – to carry the shoe between the horse and his forge. By trying the hot shoe on to the horse's foot he can tell by where it sears the horn what adjustments are necessary. When he is satisfied that the shoe is a correct fit it is cooled by being plunged into a bucket of cold water. It is then ready for nailing on.

To do this the blacksmith usually starts with the holes at the toe and works round the shoe. The nails used are of a special kind of texture, with heads which have been shaped in such a way that they will always fill the nail hole, even when the shoe is being worn away. The blacksmith is always careful as to how high he drives the nails into the wall of the foot, and as he does so he twists off the sharp end of the nail, leaving a small piece projecting through the wall known as a clench. He then knocks down the clips of the shoe on to the hoof to help hold the shoe in place. He is

Above, left: the hot shoe, carried by a pritchel, is placed against the sole. The scorch marks will show the blacksmith whether or not any final adjustments are to be made. *Left:* the shoe is fitted by nailing on, and the clenches – the ends of the nails which will come through the wall of the foot – are 'wrung-off' (*Above*).

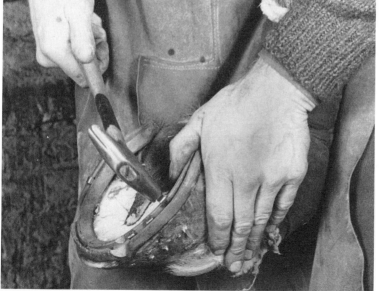

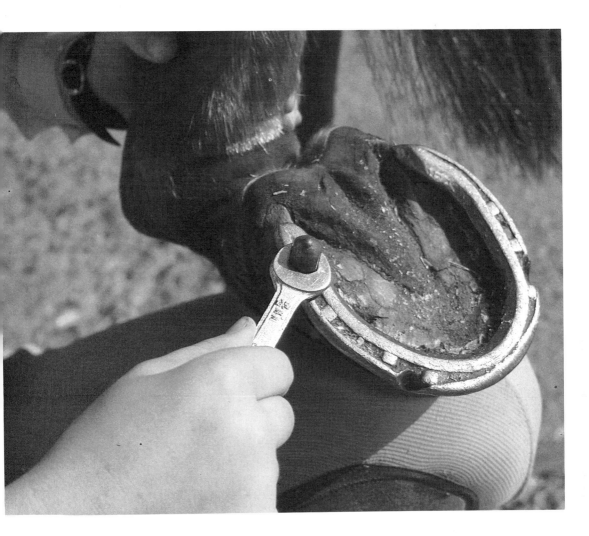

Above: horses used for jumping sometimes have specially made shoes. These have additional holes into which studs can be fitted to give added grip. Studs, made in a variety of different shapes and styles, are screwed into the shoe, but must be removed immediately the horse has finished jumping.

then ready to tidy up the clenches with his rasp, and make a small groove or bed for them in the wall so they can then be hammered down out of harm's way.

The part where the horn and shoe meet is given a final run round with a rasp, and the toe clip is given a light tap to make sure it is in the correct position. Front shoes usually have one toe clip, and hind shoes have two quarter clips to give greater security.

If the horse is to be used for jumping, the heels of the shoes may have been provided with additional holes to take heel studs. These are made of special metal in varius shapes, and screw into the shoes to give greater grip on take off and landing. They should be removed after the horse has finished jumping, and put away ready for further use.

Frequent shoeing is essential if a horse is to be kept in regular work. This will probably mean a visit from the blacksmith at least once a month. Even ponies turned out for long periods regularly need their feet trimmed.

15
Exercising

BEFORE SETTING OFF on any sort of exercise always ensure that your horse is perfectly sound and healthy. Feel his legs for any sign of heat or swelling as this will indicate signs of strain which could become worse after more work. If there is any swelling trot him up in hand and if he is sound then give him half an hour's gentle walking. If the swelling remains or he is lame then it is advisable to consult a veterinary surgeon.

Correct exercising is very important and should always be allied to the animal's state of fitness. Overworking an unfit, out of condition horse or pony can lead to lameness, respiratory and heart problems, while a fit stabled horse will become difficult to manage if not given enough exercise.

When setting off on a hack, always start off slowly and give your horse time to settle down and become accustomed to your weight on his back. You should always walk for the first ten minutes so that your horse can loosen up and stretch his muscles. In cold weather it is advisable to walk for longer as they are often stiff and more prone to muscle strain.

Once you and your horse or pony have loosened up, you can begin trotting. If you are on the roads, don't trot too fast and

never trot downhill as some roads can be very slippery. Ride on grass verges whenever practical, and where local by-laws allow, providing they are wide enough, but never canter on them. Even the quietest horse could be startled by a sudden movement in a hedge and shy into the road, possibly causing an accident. Take care to keep off verges which are obviously cared for and do not ride on footpaths.

If you can find an area of grassland which provides good going, canter work helps to clear the wind, providing your horse has achieved the necessary degree of fitness. Never canter in the same place every time because your horse will start to anticipate and become over-excited. Many horses automatically start to jog every time their feet touch grass, usually because they have been allowed to gallop on every available stretch of turf. Making your horse walk and trot in places where you sometimes canter will make him realise that being on grass is not necessarily a signal to gallop.

It is not necessary to gallop your horse or pony more than once or twice a week in order to keep him fit and when you do make sure you have plenty of room to pull up at the other end. It is always a good idea to find a gentle uphill slope if possible for any fast work as it will not only help to develop his muscles but will also make him easier to stop.

Try and vary your rides as much as possible to prevent your horse getting stale. Keeping his interest will help to prevent him becoming nappy or disobedient as these problems often arise through boredom.

Use your local bridleways as it is important to keep them open. If they run over farmland, always keep to the tracks and never ride over crops or gallop over grass fields when it is wet. Make sure you close gates properly and do not upset any livestock. Animals and crops are a farmer's livelihood so always take care not to cause any damage.

If most of your exercising has to be done on the road try and keep to quiet roads and avoid peak traffic times. If you know your horse is nervous or traffic shy, or you are riding a youngster, only go out accompanied by a quiet horse and avoid main roads.

When riding on the roads, concentrate all the time and be alert for any possible dangers. Watch for vehicles in both directions and try to avoid difficult situations – the highway is no place to teach your horse discipline. Keep to the correct side of the road and ride straight. Remember that you are not the only person using the road so always make people aware of your intentions with clear hand signals.

Look behind and in front when you want to pass a stationary vehicle and only proceed if the road is clear. Watch carefully for

Far left: a good exercise for a horse or pony is to use, whenever possible, upward sloping or hilly land. *Left:* exercise on roads or firm paths is an excellent way of building muscles – not all slow work should be done in the paddock! *Below left:* both horse and rider are enjoying their gallop during an exercise period. *Below:* gentle walking in the paddock.

any sudden movements such as a door opening or goods being unloaded, and give the vehicle plenty of clearance. If you have to pass a vehicle or an object by the side of the road and your horse will not go forward, get another horse to give you a lead. If you are by yourself and your horse resolutely refuses to pass the hazard, then as a last resort, dismount and lead him past, placing yourself between the horse and the traffic and only proceeding when the road is clear.

When turning right or left or crossing over at a junction, always give clear hand signals and wait until you have the right of way. Remember that some motorists are not immediately aware of horses so make sure you are clearly visible and never make a move until it is safe to do so.

When riding in groups, keep in pairs with a minimum of 1.5m (4ft), nose to tail, between horses. Young horses and inexperienced riders should be kept on the inside with a quieter horse between them and the traffic. Do not obstruct other road users and if the road is narrow, adopt single file once the motorist has seen the horses and slowed down. A large group of riders should split into groups with a minimum of 17m (50ft) between them so that vehicles do not have to overtake a number of animals at once, which could be dangerous in heavy traffic.

Try to avoid riding in the dark or when there are foggy conditions, but if such action is necessary it is vital to wear items of reflective material and use stirrup lights. Avoid slippery road surfaces at all times and if you are forced to exercise on icy roads, be prepared to dismount and lead your horse if conditions become extreme.

Always acknowledge any consideration shown to you by motorists, pedestrians, other riders and any other road users. A smile and a thank you costs nothing even if your horse is unworried by traffic, show your appreciation to any motorist who slows down. The day may come when you are riding a nervous horse and you will be very grateful to the drivers who slow down.

Before venturing onto the roads with any animal it would be advisable to familiarise yourself with the Highway Code and to read the booklet published by the British Horse Society, entitled *Ride and Drive Safely*.

Always remember   BE SEEN : BE IN CONTROL : BE SAFE

When returning from exercise, always make sure that your horse is cool and, if you have been galloping, that he is not blowing. If he has not settled on the way home and is still sweating when you reach the stable, walk him around until he is quiet and dry.

Top: the more competent of two riders should allow a young horse and less experienced rider to be on the inside. Both riders should be attentive and listen, with the one on the outside frequently checking what is approaching from behind. *Middle:* give correct and clear signals when you overtake. *Bottom:* get into single file when overtaking a stationary car. The more experienced rider, wearing a tabard, should not be leading in situations like this.

16
Competitive riding

THE INCREASE IN THE POPULARITY of riding has led to many more opportunities for everyone to enjoy the fun of competing. There are now different events which cater for almost every type of animal and any standard of rider. Showjumping and horse trials are attracting more support than ever, but there has also been an increase in the number of people wishing to become involved in dressage, driving, showing, team cross country, hunter trials, mounted games, polo, and endurance and long distance riding.

Any form of competition is good experience and there are now such a variety of equestrian activities that it is possible to achieve success at one or other of them, whether you enjoy jumping, dressage or riding across country.

Winning is not everything and, above all, competitions should be fun. Satisfaction comes from knowing that horse and rider have done their best on the day and were fully prepared for the demands of the event.

No form of competition should be attempted until both horse and rider have achieved the necessary degree of fitness. Asking an animal to work before it is fully fit can lead to serious injury, and in some cases, permanent damage.

When a horse or pony has spent weeks out in the field, without being ridden it becomes 'soft' and needs plenty of gentle exercise to build up its muscles, just as an athlete has to gradually build up strength and stamina. Always start by walking on the roads, to harden the horses legs and begin to turn flab into muscle. Short periods of trotting can be introduced after two weeks, but never trot too fast on hard surfaces because this can lead to jarring in the feet and legs.

Some horses require more work than others in order to attain the same degree of fitness. A big, heavy boned horse, for example, will need to do more slow work than a smaller, lighter framed horse, before starting more strenuous activity. Each horse must be treated as an individual, but if in any doubt, always stop if you think you've done enough because it is better to do too little than too much.

Whatever discipline you are interested in, regular flatwork will

Below: being out with a group is one of the great pleasures to be had from riding. All ages will enjoy themselves, especially if their journey takes them through some of the lovely Cotswold countryside shown here.

improve not only your own riding but also the performance of your horse. Schooling makes a horse more obedient and consequently easier to control. It also helps to improve balance, which in turn improves it's jumping ability. Being able to approach a jump in a controlled, steady manner will usually provide more successful results than being forced into tackling an obstacle with a headlong dash.

Schooling sessions should take place regularly, but should never be too prolonged. Twenty minutes three times a week is better than one weekly session of more than an hour. Horses are similar to children in that they have a short concentration span and are easily bored, so try and vary the work as much as possible. Always allow plenty of time for loosening up before the real work begins. It is a good idea to let your horse trot round on a loose rein for ten minutes, not only to stretch the muscles but also to relax him and get rid of any initial freshness.

Once you start working, be firm and positive and make sure that the horse realises what is required of him. Vary the pace and direction to keep him attentive, and try and avoid doing the same thing over and over again. If he starts to misbehave tell him off, but remember to praise him when he does as you ask. One smack with the stick will make the horse realise he is doing something wrong. Remember the golden rule is never lose your temper or you will achieve nothing.

Schooling over jumps should always be preceded by some flatwork and then start with just a few small, simple fences to warm up both you and the horse. Once again, the same principles apply. Don't jump the same fence over and over again, and try and use as many different types of obstacle as possible. Don't confine your schooling at home to the type of competition you are aiming for. Showjumpers can benefit from a change in routine and often enjoy practising over small cross country fences, while even some of the top show and dressage trainers include jumping as part of their horses training.

Most horses enjoy jumping, but they can become stale, so confine practising to the minimum. Always end on a good note and it is best to finish the session with an easy fence. This helps to increase the horse's confidence and leaves him with a happy memory of the lesson.

Don't try and teach the horse more than one thing in any schooling period, because this will only confuse him and lead to misunderstandings. If an animal is not doing as he is asked it is often because he doesn't understand, so always ask yourself if you are giving him clear and correct aids. Some horses learn quicker than others, so be patient if your horse is slow to realise what is required. Always reward him for trying as this will help to

establish the lesson, and never continue once the horse is tired. Their muscles begin to ache, just as ours do and asking him to work when tired will make him resentful and only encourage resitance.

The level of fitness required of you and your horse will depend on the type of competition you are intending to enter, but the build up to any event, if it is the first of the season, should take at least six weeks. This will allow for a gradual fittening programme aimed at conditioning the horse's legs, heart and lungs. After four weeks of walking and trotting followed by a further two weeks of cantering, most horses should be ready to take part in dressage or show jumping classes. Training for cross country events will take

longer because horses have to be galloping fit and able to cope with longer distances.

Galloping should only begin when the horse can canter for at least a mile without blowing. There is no short cut to fitness and if you try to do too much too soon, you will probably end up with a lame horse and nothing to ride. Horses are most susceptible to injury when they are tired and under strain so never ask them to do more than they are ready for.

Any sort of competitive outing needs planning well in advance. Decide what type of event you and your horse are most suited for and then, having sent off for the schedule and entry form, check

Above: a successful and winning combination. Lucy Sandison on Botingelle Kingfisher shows how pleased she is to have won a show pony championship.

that you are qualified to enter. Most competitions require you to enter sometime beforehand, so bear this in mind when planning your campaign.

Make a note of the date and location and if you are having to hire a horse box for the day, do so in plenty of time because they may all get booked up, particularly during the height of the season. Make sure that your horse is good to box because there is nothing more annoying than having trouble getting him to load on the morning of a competition.

A few days before the event, make a list of everything you will need to take and ensure that you have all the necessary equipment. If it is a competition involving dressage, be sure that you know the test and that you have learnt the right one! Avoid practising the whole test with your horse too often, or he will begin to anticipate your directions. Just run through the individual movements and go through the order in your mind.

Cross country courses can usually be walked the day before, but showjumping courses must be walked on the day in the time allowed by the judges before each class.

The amount of work needed by a horse on the day before a competition can vary because some horses go better when fresh, whereas others need plenty of work to keep them well behaved and obedient. As a rule, a period of light exercise is usually enough to ensure that your horse will be in good form on the day.

Give him an extra thorough grooming and see that all your tack and clothing is really clean. Gather all your equipment together and make a final check before setting off. Plenty of water and a hay net for the return journey will be necessary, and it is always a good idea to take a spare headcollar and rope in case either should break during the journey or at the competition.

A small veterinary first aid kit is also useful to take, which should include an antiseptic spray, bandages, cotton wool and a ready made poultice. A veterinary surgeon is usually present at most events so if you are at all worried about your horse while you are there, the secretary will be able to summon him for you.

On the day of the competition, leave yourself plenty of time to get ready and don't unsettle your horse by rushing round trying to do everything at the last minute. It is very important that he has plenty of time to digest his feed, and if you have a very early start or a long journey, only give him a small amount.

Bandage his legs and tail to protect him while travelling and always allow an extra half an hour for the journey in case of heavy traffic. Try to arrive at least an hour before the start of your class and go straight to the secretary's office to pick up your number and check that there have been no alterations made to your particular event.

Decide how long you will need for warming up but don't forget that your horse will probably take longer to settle than at home, so allow plenty of time for him to take in the new surroundings. Let him walk round on a loose rein until he has relaxed enough to pay attention, before starting to work him seriously. If your horse is properly fit you will not be able to tire him out before the class, and that in any case would be a waste of time as he would then be unable to perform to the best of his ability. Concentrate on settling him and gaining his attention and try to ride him as you would at home.

A number of cross country events issue individual starting times, as do dressage classes, but always check that the proceedings are running to time. If it is a showjumping class, competitors must give their number to the ring steward before the class and then wait their turn. Find out when you can walk the course and do so carefully, paying particular attention to the position of the fences and the distances between them.

Give your horse several practise jumps just to loosen him up but don't overjump him or overface him. Ten minutes before a class is not the time or place to see how high he can jump!

If you are fortunate enough to jump a clear round and qualify for a jump off, make sure you know which fences have to be jumped and work out the quickest and safest route for your horse.

Once your class is over take your horse back to the box or horse lines, remove his tack and if necessary wash him down. If he has just been across country walk him around until he has stopped blowing, before giving him a small drink of water. Don't allow him to eat until at least half an hour after his breathing has returned to normal, and give him several small drinks of water rather than allowing him to drink a whole bucket all at once.

When you are finished for the day, bandage him up, put on his rug and give him another drink of water before loading him up for the journey home. Remember that winning isn't everything and never take your disappointment out on your horse – there's always another day.

Half the fun of competing is just taking part and so try and get experience in as many different types of event as possible. Most horses are more suited to one discipline than another but time spent on one activity can improve their performance in another. Horses that lack the natural paces to do well at dressage, may be very good jumpers, while those that are very bold and brave across country may be too careless when it comes to showjumping. To enjoy success in any equestrian sport first decide what your horse is best suited to, or alternatively, choose the event you most enjoy and then find a horse with the necessary requirements.

Above: dressage at all levels is becoming an increasingly popular equestrian activity, whether competing in a dressage test, or carrying out the test as one phase of horse trials.

Dressage

In dressage competitions, horses must perform a test involving set movements at walk, trot and canter. Each movement is marked out of 10, with extra points awarded for freedom and regularity of paces, impulsion, obedience, acceptance of the bridle, position of the rider and correct use of the aids. Horses should be supple and well balanced with good natural paces, calm and well schooled.

A smart appearance helps create a picture of harmony and is also courteous to the judges. Horses should be plaited and ridden in either a snaffle or a simple double bridle, unless stated otherwise in the rules. Whips and martingales are not allowed, and neither are boots or bandages, although these may be worn while warming up.

Showing

There are many different types of show classes ranging from small ponies to heavyweight hunters, but all require a well mannered horse with good conformation. All competitors enter the ring simultaneously and consequently a good show horse must be well behaved in company and willing to stand quietly in a line if necessary.

Some classes, working hunters for example, require the horse to jump a short course, although this is always stated in the schedule. Although conformation, turnout and movement are very important, there are shows which provide classes for 'family ponies' aimed at the more versatile animal which, as the name suggests, can be ridden by children or adults and is a safe, enjoyable ride.

Sometimes the judge will ride several of the horses in the final line-up and, as this can affect the placings, it is important that the animal is both comfortable and obedient and does not become upset when ridden by a stranger.

Above: note the determination in this young rider's face when tackling this ascending spread obstacle.

Show jumping

Show jumping requires a horse or pony that is obedient, careful and clever, with the agility to turn quickly, and the scope to jump different types of obstacles. Accuracy and control are vital for success in competitions, especially those in which one hundredth of a second can make the difference between winning and finishing in second place.

If you wish to start show jumping, an experienced horse or pony is almost as important as a good instructor, but in the end there is no substitute for competitive experience. Some horses

Below: Sally Mapleson who has represented Great Britain on several occasions, seen here on Chinatown.

Left: a young rider jumping a fallen tree, one of the testing obstacles frequently found in hunter trials.

Above: Gillian Greenwood, one of the most successful young riders, is seen here with her horse, Sky Fly.

tend to become sour when over-jumped. This can be avoided by careful planning of entries to competitions. When buying a horse or pony for show jumping be sure it is being sold for a genuine reason and not because it has lost enthusiasm.

Never over-face a young horse in the ring, and try not to go too fast when jumping 'against the clock' until you both have the necessary confidence and ability. Remember, show jumping demands accuracy and that this is sometimes more important than speed.

Eventing

Eventing, or horse trials, to use the new accepted name, are becoming increasingly popular at all levels, and can be looked upon as the true test of the complete horseman. In the past, event riders have been called 'jacks of all trades and masters of none', but competing in horse trials demands a high degree of skill from horse and rider in all three phases: dressage, show jumping and riding cross country.

There are two main types of horse trials – one day events and three day events. In a one day trial, competitors must perform a dressage test, jump a round of show jumps and then negotiate a cross country course which could be over two and a half miles in length and contain more than 20 fences, with only a short break in between each phase.

A three day event always begins with a veterinary inspection of all the horses, followed the next day by the dressage phase. The speed and endurance consists of the first set of roads and tracks and then the steeplechase, when competitors have to negotiate up to two miles and ten chase fences at racing pace. The second and longer set of roads and tracks should then be covered mainly at a steady trot, after which horses get a ten minute rest before setting off on the four mile cross country course.

The next day there is a further veterinary examination before the final showjumping phase.

Left: two happy competitors approaching a ford in a Golden Horse Shoe Ride.

Below: the Golden Horse Shoe Ride, one of the newest of equestrian activities.

Top class three day events require a horse that is bold, obedient, well schooled, has the ability to jump fences at speed and the agility to cope with awkward combinations, and is above all tough and sound. They should ideally be at least three-quarter Thoroughbred to enable them to have the necessary speed and the stamina to keep galloping over long distances. The smaller events, however, can be great fun and are good experience for both horse and rider as the emphasis is on all round ability rather than excellence in any one field.

Above: another view of young riders competing in a Golden Horse Shoe Ride in 1985.

Hunter Trials

Hunter trials are very good training grounds for potential event horses, where they can be introduced to all sorts of natural fences. Courses are usually rather more straightforward than those built for horse trials and sometimes involve the opening and closing of a gate, during a timed section.

A number of horses that dislike showjumping or have become bored and stale often regain their enthusiasm going across country, while others lack the necessary boldness to enjoy jumping ditches, banks and drops.

Team Cross Country

Team cross country is one of the fastest growing equestrian sports in Britain and is attracting a great deal of financial support. They are ideal events for encouraging young horses, provided they are not taken too fast too soon. Each team consists of three or four riders who must negotiate the course together. In most classes the fastest team wins, having been timed from when the leading rider goes through the start and the last of the team having crossed the finish.

The obstacles found in cross-country competitions are usually of a fixed nature, and tackling a cross-country course involves a different approach to that used when show jumping.

Above: Pony Club Mounted Games at the Horse of the Year Show and about to change-over in the baton relay in one of competitions staged by the Pony Club.

Gymkhana Events

The most popular classes at most local shows are the gymkhana events. Bending races, sack, races, egg and spoon races are just some of the events which young riders can enjoy. Unlike showing and jumping, this is the sport where an average pony can excell, but a good temperament is necessary to cope with the hustle and bustle and the noise which always surrounds the proceedings.

These events have become so popular that there are now competitions for teams of riders, known as Mounted Games.

Driving

Show driving and driving trials have become increasingly well
supported in recent years and many young people are starting to
take an active interest in driving. It is a sport which demands a
high degree of skill and driving trials in particular require a cool
head and quick reactions.

There are now courses available for beginners and anyone
interested in learning how to drive should seek advice from a
professional because it can be a dangerous sport for the
inexperienced.

Long Distance Riding

Long Distance and Endurance Riding provide opportunities for all ages of rider to compete. The most suitable horses are usually under 15.2hh, many of the best being from a native pony crossed with a Thoroughbred or Arab. They are consequently less expensive to buy and relatively economical to keep compared with some of the other competition horses.

Competitors require a high standard of horse-mastership to produce their horses fit enough to pass the stringent veterinary examinations that take place on all rides at the start, finish and along the route.

Glossary

AGED when a horse is seven years old or more.

ANTICAST ROLLER OR ARCH ROLLER a type of stable roller which has a metal arch to prevent the horse from rolling over in his box.

APRON-FACED a horse which has a large white mark on his face.

ARCH-MOUTH PELHAM a pelham bit which has a mouthpiece with an upward curve.

ARTZEL a white mark on the forehead of a horse.

ATHERSTONE GIRTH usually made of baghide leather and shaped to give extra movement at the horse's elbows to prevent any chafing.

BANBURY MOUTHPIECE a mouthpiece of a bit which has a rounded bar which is tapered in the centre and fitted into slots in the cheekpieces.

BARREL a horseshoe which has a metal piece welded across the heel to give additional support. By placing additional pressure on the horse's frog it can provide relief if a horse has corns or sidebones.

BEHIND THE BIT when a horse refuses to take a proper hold of his bit.

BIB MARTINGALE a running Martingale with a triangular leather centrepiece.

BITLESS BRIDLE a bridle without a bit which acts on the chin and nose carriage.

BLAIR BRIDLE a type of bitless bridle with long cheekpieces.

BLAZE a white marking on a horse extending the full length of the face.

BLEMISH any scar left by an injury or wound which does not affect a horse's performance or health.

BLOOD HORSE an English Thoroughbred.

BOG SPAVIN a soft non-painful swelling on the inside and slightly to the front of the hock joint.

BONE SPAVIN a hard bony swelling on the inside lower edge of the hock joint.

BORE when a horse leans on the bit.

BREAK OUT when a horse sweats suddenly.

BRUSHING the act of a horse striking the inside of one leg near the fetlock joint, with the opposite hoof or shoe (also known as cutting).

BRUSHING BOOTS usually made of leather or felt with a padded portion running down the inside to give protection to the joints if a horse strokes one leg against another.

CADE FOAL a foal reared by hand.

CAMP when a horse stands with his fore and hind legs spread as far apart as possible.

CANKER a morbid growth of the horn on the foot.

CANNON BONE the solid bone between the knee and the fetlock of a horse. It should be short for strength and look flat from the side.

CAPPED HOCK a swelling on the joint of the hock usually caused through shortage of bedding or when a horse is travelling.

CAST when a horse loses a shoe; when hounds attempt to regain the scent of their quarry at a check, or when a horse lies down in his box and is unable to get up usually because of an obstruction in the box.

CHANGE LEADS when a horse changes the leading leg when cantering or galloping.

CHANGE OF LEG a movement in cantering when a horse is made to lead with the other leg.

CINCH UP an American term for fastening the girth of a horse.

CLENCH the pointed end of a nail which protrudes through the hoof after a horse has been shod (sometimes called a Clinch).

COLIC pain in the digestive organs of a horse.

COLT an ungelded male horse less than four years old.

CONTACT the link which the hands of a rider have with a horse's mouth through the reins.

COW HOCKS hocks which turn inwards.

CRACKED HEELS inflammation of the skin in the hollow of the horse's heel.

CRIB BITING a bad vice in horses where a horse bites his crib or some other protection and at the same time swallows air. This habit is frequently started by boredom and is usually associated with wind-sucking.

DRESSAGE a series of exercises to show a horse's obedience to his rider's commands.

DROPPED NOSE-BAND a nose band sometimes used with a snaffle bit to prevent a horse from opening his mouth too wide or allowing the bit to slide to one side.

ELECTUARY the term used for a medicine for horses in which the drugs are made into a paste with a base of treacle or honey.

FROG the V-shaped formation in the sole of a horse's foot.

FROG-CLEFT the natural depression in the centre of the frog at the widest part.

FULL-MOUTH a horse at six years old.

FULLERING a groove in the ground surface of a horse shoe in which the nail holes are placed.

FULMER SNAFFLE a cheek snaffle fitted with a broad jointed mouthpiece and loose rings (sometimes called an Australian Horse Ring Snaffle).

GALL a sore place caused by badly fitting saddlery, usually found under the girth of a saddle particularly when a horse is in soft condition.

GIRTH SLEEVE a sleeve of sheepskin or rubber which passes over the girth to prevent galling.

GIVE WITH THE HAND opening the fingers sufficiently to relax the tension of the reins.

GONE IN THE WIND a term applied to any affection of a horse's wind, and indicates that the horse is of 'unsound wind'.

HAND the measurement by which the height of a horse or pony is calculated – 10cm (4 in).

KNEE SPAVIN a bony growth at the back of the knee.

MUD FEVER inflamation of the heels, legs or belly.

OVER-REACHING when the toe of the hind shoe strikes against the heel of the forefeet.

ROLLER a form of girth made of leather, webbing or hemp to keep a rug in place.

RUGGING UP a term used for putting rugs on a horse.

SADDLE-HORSE a wooden stand upon which saddles can be placed for cleaning or storage.

SADDLE SOAP a specially prepared soap which is applied with a damp sponge for cleaning saddles, bridles and other leather harness.

SIDE BONE a hard lump on the coronet on either side of the heel.

SPLINT a small bony growth between the splint bone and the cannon bone.

TEMPERATURE the normal temperature of a horse is 38°C (100.5°F).

TENDON BOOTS specially designed boots, usually of leather, which protect the tendons.

WOLF TEETH rudimentary teeth in front of the upper and lower molar teeth.

Index